Nature at Your Doorstep

NATURE AT YOUR DOORSTEP

Real World Investigations
for Primary Students

Carole G. Basile

Jennifer Gillespie-Malone

Fred Collins

Illustrated by

Sabra Booth

In conjunction with the
Hana and Arthur Ginzbarg Nature Discovery Center
Bellaire, Texas

1997
TEACHER IDEAS PRESS
A Division of
Libraries Unlimited, Inc.
Englewood, Colorado

To all children, past, present, and future,
who explore and discover
nature at their doorstep.

———————

TEACHER IDEAS PRESS
A Division of
Libraries Unlimited, Inc.
P.O. Box 6633
Englewood, CO 80155-6633
1-800-237-6124

Production Editor: Kay Mariea
Copy Editor: Aviva Rothschild
Proofreader: Susie Sigman
Design and Layout: Pamela J. Getchell

Library of Congress Cataloging-in-Publication Data

Basile, Carole G., 1958-
    Nature at your doorstep : real world investigations for primary
students / Carole G. Basile, Jennifer Gillespie-Malone, Fred Collins ;
illustrated by Sabra Booth ; in conjunction with the Hana and
Arthur Ginzbarg Nature Discovery Center.
    xxvi, 161 p. 22x28 cm.
    Includes bibliographical references.
    ISBN 1-56308-455-4
    1. Ecology--Study and teaching--Activity programs. 2. Nature
study--Activity programs. I. Gillespie-Malone, Jennifer, 1949-
II. Collins, Fred, 1949-   . III. Hana and Arthur Ginzbarg Nature
Discovery Center. IV. Title.
QH541.2.B38 1997
372.3'57044--dc21   96-39312
                                                              CIP

CONTENTS

PREFACE

Nature at Your Doorstep is an outgrowth of a successful environmental education program at the Hana and Arthur Ginzbarg Nature Discovery Center in Bellaire, Texas. Hana and Arthur Ginzbarg felt that for many people nature can be the ultimate educator and comforter. They dedicated their lives to saving pearls of nature for everyone to enjoy. The center named in their honor continues their dream of bringing people and nature together. The mission statement conveys this sentiment best:

> To kindle urban dwellers' curiosity about the interdependent world of nature of which we are a part, and to foster through education, responsibility toward our environment.

To help accomplish this mission, the Nature Discovery Center began hosting school field trips in 1990. We wanted to kindle curiosity and wonder about nature, but first we had to show urban children that nature was real, not just on the Discovery Channel or compact discs, and especially not just in Africa or South America. We found that inner-city students often asked, "What are those rats with fuzzy tails?" as we watched squirrels scampering along the ground. We became increasingly aware that students really need to find nature at their doorstep if we are to begin changing some prevalent misconceptions.

By interacting personally with the students, exploring the park's tiny habitats, and listening to students' questions, we realized that the basics of biology could even be grasped by young children. They *could* understand the concepts of behavior and function, and a plant or animal's place in the environment. Emphasis on increasing children's awareness of the natural world became an important focus for the center. Nature walks with small groups of students focused on a variety of topics. This early program typically involved a docent pointing out whatever was of interest that day. Student data sheets consisted of tally sheets for counting the animals commonly found in the park.

As the program continued, we adapted the scientific method to provide logic and structure to the outdoor experience. Each investigation posed a question to the visiting students, who then developed their own hypotheses, collected and recorded data, and drew conclusions. Investigations usually focused on birds or squirrels. On cold days, when animals seemed scarce, we focused on senses. We added new investigations, such as habitats, which allowed students to place animals in context; biodiversity; food webs; ecological communities; and endangered species so that students might comprehend more complex topics.

The approach proved tremendously effective for students and appreciated by teachers. Several thousand students were participating in the program over the year, and demand for the program created a waiting list. Our facility was at maximum capacity, yet only a tiny fraction of our service area population was able to attend. We needed to expand the program by providing students with similar experiences in their own schoolyards.

Therefore, we focused on strengthening the availability and credibility of the program. We offered teacher workshops and presented our program at local, regional, and national education meetings and conferences. In addition, an experimental research study (Basile 1996) was conducted with third grade students. The study indicated that students who had worked with the *Nature at Your Doorstep* program could transfer content and process knowledge to new problem situations better than those who had learned in a traditional classroom setting. Because of these efforts, we have received numerous requests to assist schools in implementing this program.

In response, we created this book to share our program with teachers both in and out of our community. We have compiled those investigation topics that can be studied at any schoolyard site across the country, and we hope teachers will enjoy the same success with their students that we have had with ours. With your participation, we believe this program can impart critical thinking, problem-solving skills, and logic to today's students, so that they can learn about wildlife and its needs and become better stewards of tomorrow's environment.

ACKNOWLEDGMENTS

We would like to acknowledge the following people and corporations that have contributed to the program over the years to make it what it is today.

Hana and Arthur Ginzbarg

Past and Present Staff Members:

Mary Ann Beauchemin, Anne Eisner, Melissa Geis,
Kelly Levitt, Dalal Oubari, Aida Pineda, David Perry,
Nettie Ramsey, Janet Roberts, and Laura Ryder

Dedicated *Nature at Your Doorstep* Volunteers:

Kathy Brown, Edith Fulton, Mary Green, Marge Hanselman,
Janie Harris, Mary Ann Harvie, Rose Kimball, Lois Lively,
Alex Malone, Garrick Malone, Anne McIntyre, Mary Jane Peace,
Cathleen Trechter, Adrianne Weir-Villatoro, Cindy Williams

Condit Elementary School

Carol Kanewske, Martha Fields,
and the 1995-96 Third Grade Students

Program Sponsors:

BP Exploration, Powell Foundation, Compaq Foundation

INTRODUCTION

Nature at Your Doorstep is an outgrowth of a successful environmental education program currently being offered as a school field trip at the Hana and Arthur Ginzbarg Nature Discovery Center in Bellaire, Texas. It has been developed and used with thousands of students throughout Bellaire and the surrounding Houston metroplex. This program provides an opportunity for teachers to share nature with their students in ways that promote discovery and problem solving.

PURPOSE

In keeping with the mission of the Nature Discovery Center, the purpose of this program is to kindle students' curiosity and wonder about the interdependent world of nature of which we are a part, and to foster through education, their responsibility toward our environment.

GOALS AND OBJECTIVES

The National Science Education Standards (National Research Council 1996) propose that learning about science is something that students do, not something that is done to them. Students must have minds-on experiences, not just hands-on experiences. Therefore, each unit is designed to guide students through the discovery of basic biological concepts using the scientific method as a logical method of inquiry. Students will explore questions, formulate hypotheses based on their current knowledge, collect data relevant to the questions, and, by creating various forms of representations, analyze their data to formulate conclusions and compare those conclusions to their hypotheses. In addition, students will demonstrate learning through a variety of mathematical and language arts skills.

CHILDREN AS SCIENTISTS

All children are scientists. Their natural curiosity, ability to pose questions without hesitation, and acute observational skills make them some of the best scientists around. If this natural talent is encouraged at an early age, then by learning scientific content and processes they can learn in the environment, about the environment, for the environment (Murdoch 1995).

With *Nature at Your Doorstep*, students can be anything from botanists studying plants to wildlife biologists studying endangered species. Most importantly, they can do it all within their schoolyard. Students investigate and evaluate situations and learn strategies for ensuring that the balance of nature is maintained.

OVERVIEW OF THE UNITS AND THEIR COMPONENTS

Where to Start

There are 10 units in the book: *Senses, Trees, Birds, Insects and Neighbors, Ants, Biodiversity, Habitats, Communities, Food Webs*, and *Endangered Species*. We suggest beginning with Senses. Everyone who embarks on the exploration of the outdoors needs to be aware of their senses. A strong emphasis here will enhance learning and discovery in every other unit.

Following Senses, units may be done randomly, as your curriculum dictates, except for Food Webs and Endangered Species. In order to do Food Webs, students should have completed Biodiversity or Communities. In order to do Endangered Species, students should have at least completed Habitats, Communities, and Food Webs. These prerequisites allow students to internalize concepts of food webs and endangered species and to relate them to their own schoolyard environment.

Components of Each Unit

Each unit consists of two components. First, every unit provides focus and background material, activities to introduce the topic, suggestions for teaching each of the data sheets, and extensions for further study. Suggestions for teaching the program are based on the authors' experience at the nature center and local schools. Second, student data sheet masters are included so that teachers may reproduce them for each student or simply use them as a guide for group investigations. All the units are integrated with opportunities for learning experiences in science, mathematics, and language arts. Depending on the age of your students and your focus, you may want to use all or just some of the data sheets provided in each unit.

Introduction Sheet

This sheet has three parts: *What's Happening, Schoolyard Challenge*, and *Rhonda's Word Play*. (See page xv for example.) In What's Happening, students begin their journey by reading background information about the topic they will investigate. Schoolyard Challenge directs them to become scientists by presenting a series of questions and encouraging them to begin their explorations. In Rhonda's Word Play, Rhonda suggests a language activity that provides students with challenges such as writing poems, decoding messages, or creating word trees. Each word play is associated with the topic to further excite students' interest.

Investigating

The Investigation sheets provide the basis for each investigation. (See page xvi for example.) Students write variables, review the research question, make hypotheses, collect data, and formulate conclusions. In some units, two Investigation sheets are provided. Use the one you feel is most appropriate for your students' abilities. These sheets can be used repeatedly at different times of the day or year or at different sites. Have your students keep a notebook with their investigations so they can see their progress as scientists.

NATURE AT YOUR DOORSTEP

Spotlighting Senses

What's Happening

Scientists are people who ask questions such as "What makes the sun hot?" "Why do things fall down but not up?" "How do birds sing?" "Why do frogs lay eggs in water?" Scientists want to learn about the world in as many ways as they can. They use their *senses* of sight, hearing, smell, and touch.

Schoolyard Challenge

Your challenge is to be a scientist. You will learn about nature in your schoolyard by using your senses. Ask yourself some questions about learning with your senses. What senses will I use in my schoolyard today? What can I learn using my ears? What can I discover using my nose?

EXTRA! Rhonda's Word Play

The word "sense" is a homonym with the word "cents" and "scents." That means they sound the same. Can you think of any other "senses" words that have homonyms?

NATURE AT YOUR DOORSTEP

TREES
INVESTIGATION

Investigator _Scott Reynolds_
Date _____
Time _____
Weather _Sunny to Partly cloudy_
Study area _Park_

QUESTION: What kind of trees will I find today?

HYPOTHESES: I **think** that I will find trees with these shapes:

I **think** I will find leaves with these shapes:

I **think** I will find a bark that feels: ☑ rough, ☑ smooth, ☑ bumpy,
❑ _____.

DATA:

Tree shapes: *Fill in one box for each tree that matches the shape picture.*

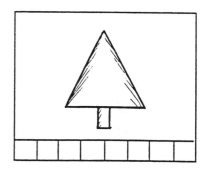 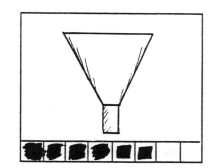 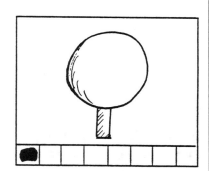

Leaf shapes: *Fill in one box for each tree you find with leaves that match the picture.*

Making Comparisons

A number of comparisons can be made using the data recorded on students' Investigation sheets. Use the Make a Comparison sheet to compare the students' hypotheses to their compiled data or to compare two sets of data collected from different habitats, seasons, or times of day. (See page xviii for example.)

Connecting Mathematics

Students can create their own representations of the data they have collected. (See page xix for example.) Each unit focuses on a different type of representation, such as tally charts, bar graphs, circle graphs, pictographs, Venn diagrams, or line graphs. Layouts are provided, but students should be encouraged to create their own representations as well.

Students can then analyze their representations by answering the series of questions provided. Again, depending on the age and abilities of your students, they may write the answers to these questions on their own, with a partner, or in small groups; you can also pose the questions to the group as a whole.

In addition, a problem-solving activity is included in the teacher's section to further challenge students. These are nonroutine problems that encourage students to use a variety of problem-solving strategies.

Creating Your Own Investigation

The Create Your Own Investigation sheet has been developed so that students can create their own investigation by defining their own variables, hypotheses, data collection procedures, and conclusions. (See page xx for example.) The sheet also acts as an assessment tool for determining if students can apply their knowledge in another setting, and can be used as a method of involving parents.

YOUR ROLE AS COACH

Your role as coach for these investigations is to assist your students in guided discovery, helping them use their senses to collect data, develop ideas and test them through the scientific method, and make their own discoveries. The process of investigating and working out their ideas is more important than the specific answers on each data sheet.

The most important instructional strategy for this curriculum is the use of questioning strategies. Freedman (1994) defines six types of questions:

- *Description questions* encourage students to use their senses (e.g., What does it feel like? What does it smell like?)

- *Comparison questions* encourage students to compare and contrast different things (e.g., What is the difference between . . . ? What do you see that is the same between . . . ?)

- *Analysis questions* encourage students to describe what something is and isn't (e.g., Can you tell me about what you found? What didn't you find that you thought you might?)

- *Problem-solving questions* provide opportunities to describe a problem, propose a solution, and convince a group that it is reasonable and feasible (e.g., What if . . . ? What is the problem? How might you solve it? Why do you feel your hypothesis would work?)

Text continues on page xxi.

NATURE AT YOUR DOORSTEP

MAKE A COMPARISON

My comparison is between birds and squirrels

Birdland Create-your Own,

Ellen + Jenni   Location

What is the same? (Write a sentence or draw a picture.)

Time
weather
study area

What is different? (Write a sentence or draw a picture.)

most squirrels were on the ground
Most birds were in the air

2nd most squirrels were low in bushes
2nd most birds were high in tree

NATURE AT YOUR DOORSTEP

MATH CONNECTION - TREES

Can you create a vertical bar graph for your data?
Sort your leaves by the shapes at the bottom of the graph.

Title:

Leaf Catagorizing

number of leaves

leaf shapes

ANALYZE YOUR DATA

Which leaf shape did you find the most? _____

Which leaf shape did you find the least? _____

Why? _Most of the trees contained three lobed leaves_

NATURE AT YOUR DOORSTEP

CREATE YOUR OWN

(Title) Squirrel location

INVESTIGATION

Investigator _Jennifer_
Date _5-10-96_
Time _12 noon_
Weather _hot_
Study area _Park_

QUESTION: *(What question do you have?)* Where will the squirrel be today

HYPOTHESIS: *(What is your hypothesis?)* The squirrel will be in the trees most. I think

DATA: *(How will you keep track of your data?)* Create your own data table:

Trees   0

bushes   ⊪⊦   5

groond   ⊪⊦ ⊪⊦ | 11

CONCLUSION: I found _a lot of squirrels on the looking for food_

- *Fiction questions* ask students to synthesize information in an imaginary context (e.g., If you were . . . what would you do?)

- *Evaluation questions* focus on supporting evidence, facts, expert opinion, or research (e.g., How do you know . . .? What evidence do you have that supports your hypothesis?)

If these strategies are used on a regular basis, students will spend more time on their own investigating, researching, solving problems, and drawing their own conclusions. Examples of questions are included in most sections of each unit. With practice these questions will become second nature, and the difference they can make to the students will amaze you.

Your role as a coach and facilitator will determine this program's success. We have provided this tool for you to use as a supplement to your classroom activities. Your job is to get the most out of the information within by asking good questions of your students and allowing them to make discoveries on their own. The foundations you build today can last a lifetime.

THE OUTDOOR CLASSROOM

School grounds are often an excellent mirror of the neighborhood, giving students insights into their own environment that they might not gain if they did their science work indoors or at distant sites. School grounds provide the wonder of continual discovery in a familiar and accessible setting on their home turf. Don't worry if your schoolyard does not have a large green space or an improved habitat; even a small area will provide a site big enough for viewing nature.

TIPS FOR TEACHING OUTDOORS

The outdoor classroom is a special one. The following are suggestions derived from years of experience working with students in schoolyards, parks, and nature sanctuaries.

Planning

Planning is one of the keys to effective teaching outdoors.

- Check the study area ahead of time, so you will have an idea what you might find.

- Know the objective of each unit.

- Be sure the students know what the purpose of the investigation is and how they will use their data sheets.

- Set a time frame that will fit your students' attention spans, the study topic, and the weather.

- The idea of outdoor classwork will be new to many of your students. Decide ahead of time with your class what your rules and guidelines for outdoor behavior are. For example, stay with the group or your partner, walk and talk quietly so that animals are not scared away, freeze and point when you see something interesting so that others can see it as well.

Keeping the Objective in Mind

The teaching strategy for these outdoor investigations is an exploratory or discovery approach. Students are motivated to use all of their senses for their own first-hand discoveries. A systematic use of questioning with the unit objective in mind will encourage students to think about their observations, to integrate and synthesize information, and to formulate reasonable conclusions.

Managing the Group

A number of techniques work well to keep the students' attention focused on the study topic and to keep everyone together while teaching outside.

- Before you start, at the end, or even in the middle of an investigation, you can have the group sit on the ground. With everyone together you can review the data sheets, wrap up, or find out what has been discovered up to that point.

- Always have a grabber ready for observation. Grabbers are items of focus, something to look at or listen to. Grabbers also provide an opportunity to gather the group and model the kinds of behavior you want your students to follow. A grabber may be something you find or something you bring in your pocket just in case.

- Be aware of the sun. When you stop to talk to the class in an open area, try to position yourself so that you are facing the sun and the students are not.

- Address the group from the middle. If you are leading a group along a trail, walk until about half the group is past the object or place on which you wish to focus. Stop and move to the middle of the group so the students at both ends of the line can hear and see you.

Being Flexible

An open mind, curiosity, and enthusiasm are your best tools for assisting students to investigate the outdoors. A sense of humor will also help you be flexible in your outdoor teaching. Outdoor classrooms are always open for surprises. However, surprises can easily be transformed from aggravating interruptions into teaching highs.

Take the time to watch and enjoy the phenomenon; encourage your students to observe what is happening. With flexibility and humor you can enjoy these "teachable moments" without discarding the focus of the day's topic altogether. By the time you and your students move on, you may even be able to connect the surprise to the topic at hand.

You do not need to know the answers to the questions students ask. Admit that you do not know, and look up the answers back in the classroom or on the next trip to the library. Keep a notebook in your pocket to write down the question and the student who asked.

Even when you do know the answer, it often works well to let the students discover answers for themselves by asking leading questions. Be aware that some students stop investigating things once they have a concrete answer or name for something. If a student asks what something is, you can turn the question around by asking what that student thinks it is, or what name the student would give it based on its characteristics.

STUDENTS WITH SPECIAL NEEDS

Recognizing the needs of all students in your classroom is important, especially for students with disabilities. There are two things to keep in mind: form and function.

Decide what format is appropriate for that individual student. The data sheets may need to be modified or not used at all. For example, instead of collecting color or behavior data about birds, they may simply count birds using some form of manipulative (i.e., tiles, beans, or pictures of birds).

The function of a special-needs student may be different from the function of other students. For example, while others are collecting leaves, that student may be in charge of sorting them. Keeping an open mind to alternatives will ensure these students a place in these special projects.

CURRICULUM ELEMENTS

Educational standards have been developed for a number of curriculum areas. *Nature at Your Doorstep* strongly supports the standards in science, mathematics, language arts, and social studies. The following illustrates which standards for science (NCR 1996), mathematics (NCTM 1989), language arts (IRA, NCTE 1996), and social studies (NCSS 1994) are met in these areas.

SCIENCE STANDARDS

Science as Inquiry— Abilities
- Ask a question about objects, organisms, and events in the environment.
- Plan and conduct a simple investigation.
- Employ simple equipment and tools to gather data and extend the senses.
- Use data to construct a reasonable explanation.
- Communicate investigations and explanations.

Science as Inquiry— Understandings
- Scientific investigations involve asking and answering a question and comparing the answer with what scientists already know about the world.
- Scientists use different kinds of investigations depending on the questions they are trying to answer.
- Simple instruments provide more information than scientists obtain using only their senses.
- Scientists develop explanations using observations and what they already know about the world.

Life Science— Characteristics of Organisms
- Organisms have basic needs. Organisms can survive only in environments in which their needs can be met.
- Each plant or animal has different structures that serve different functions in growth, survival, and reproduction.
- The behavior of individual organisms is influenced by internal and external cues.

Life Science— Organisms and Environments
- All animals depend on plants. Some animals eat plants for food. Other animals eat animals that eat the plants.
- An organism's patterns of behavior are related to the nature of that organism's environment.
- All organisms cause changes in the environment where they live.

MATHEMATICS STANDARDS

Mathematics as Problem Solving
- Use problem-solving approaches to investigate and understand mathematical content.
- Formulate problems from everyday and mathematical situations.
- Develop and apply strategies to solve a wide variety of problems.
- Verify and interpret results with respect to the original problem.
- Acquire confidence in using mathematics meaningfully.

Mathematics as Communication
- Relate physical materials, pictures, and diagrams to mathematical ideas.
- Reflect on and clarify thinking about mathematical ideas and situations.
- Relate everyday language to mathematical language and symbols.
- Realize that representing, discussing, reading, writing, and listening to mathematics are a vital part of learning and using mathematics.

Mathematical Connections
- Link conceptual and procedural knowledge.
- Use mathematics in other curriculum areas.
- Use mathematics in their daily lives.

Statistics and Probability
- Collect, organize, and describe data.
- Construct, read, and interpret displays of data.
- Formulate and solve problems that involve collecting and analyzing data.

LANGUAGE ARTS STANDARDS

- Students employ a wide range of strategies as they write and use different writing process elements appropriately to communicate with different audiences for a variety of purposes.

- Students conduct research on issues and interests by generating ideas and questions, and by posing problems. They gather, evaluate, and synthesize data from a variety of sources to communicate their discoveries to an audience in ways that suit their purpose.

- Students use a variety of technological and informational resources to gather and synthesize information and to create and communicate knowledge.

- Students use spoken, written, and visual language to accomplish their own purposes.

SOCIAL STUDIES STANDARDS

Time, Continuity, and Change
- Demonstrate an ability to identify examples of change.
- Recognize cause and effect relationships.

People, Places and Environments
- Examine the interaction of human beings and their physical environment, the use of land, building of cities, and ecosystem changes in selected locales and regions.

Individual Development and Identity
- Work independently and cooperatively to accomplish goals.

MATERIALS

The nice thing about *Nature at Your Doorstep* is that you do not need a lot of materials to make it work. If your students are nonwriters, then you may need only chart paper and markers to record group hypotheses, data, and conclusions, and to create your graphs. Students who can write will need:

- Clipboards (Foam core board or heavy cardboard cut into 9" x 12" pieces with rubber bands around them make great clipboards for students.)
- Pencils, crayons, or colored markers

Other materials are optional but can be helpful to have in an outdoor class backpack:

- Groundsheet for students to sit on
- Magnifying glasses
- Outdoor thermometer
- Hand net
- Specimen boxes
- Binoculars
- Litter bag

- Flashlight
- Tape measures
- Rulers
- Hand spade
- Compass
- Calculators

SAMPLE 10-DAY LESSON PLAN

This sample lesson plan may help you as you begin using *Nature at Your Doorstep*. This plan assumes approximately one hour per day for the program. However, each unit need not be done for 10 consecutive days or a full hour per day. You may be able to do parts of the program during language arts, mathematics, art, science, or wherever they fit your schedule. Also, different units take different amounts of time. As you become more familiar with each unit, you can decide what works best based on your time constraints and the level and experience of your students.

Day One   Have students read What's Happening. Use one or two of the introductory exercises to introduce the topic.

Day Two   Have students read Schoolyard Challenge. Discuss becoming a scientist. Begin a list of questions that students have about the topic. Read one of the books from the suggested children's literature.

Day Three   Discuss the variables on the Investigation sheet and students' hypotheses. Collect data in your schoolyard. Formulate conclusions.

Day Four   Compare the hypotheses to the conclusions on the Make a Comparison sheet.

Day Five   Have students create a representation of the data.

Day Six   Have students analyze the data. Provide students with the related problem-solving opportunity suggested in each Connecting Mathematics section.

Day Seven   Have a research day for students to investigate any unanswered questions they might have.

Day Eight   Collect data again in the schoolyard, making sure to change one of the variables.

Day Nine   Compare the data collected the first time to the data collected the second time. Assign the Create Your Own Investigation page for homework. Use a copy of the parent letter provided in the Appendix to get parents involved.

Day Ten   Have a show-and-tell session where students explain their variables and hypotheses, how they collected data, and their conclusions from their investigations at home.

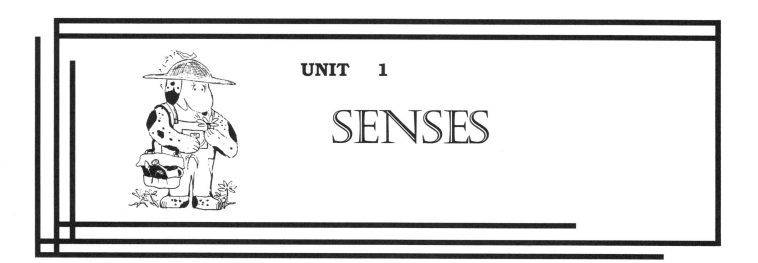

UNIT 1

SENSES

FOCUS

This investigation focuses on building heightened awareness of the things around us, both natural and human-made. Increasing students' use of their senses will help them discover new things about nature and its interactions.

BACKGROUND INFORMATION

We use our senses to tell us about the world around us. Senses provide five avenues to discovery: sight, sound, taste, touch, and smell. Often we focus so strongly on sight that we ignore what our other senses tell us. Certainly color vision is wonderful, but hearing alerts us to things all around us. Sound alerts us to danger even better than sight. That's why rattlesnakes have rattles and fire trucks have sirens.

We continually receive and use information gathered through our skin, our sense of touch. We feel cold and hot, wet and dry, and a wide variety of textures. We may be the only species of animal on earth that can recognize an object by feel.

Smell is our most neglected sense. Smell, however, conveys far more information than we realize. Watch any dog and see how it uses smell to confirm what it thinks it sees or hears. Smell is extremely important in helping us interpret the emotional state of people around us, even though we don't realize it. The perfume industry is based on this fact.

One word of caution about the sense of taste: Tasting plants or other outdoor items can be dangerous and should be discouraged. Each animal's physiology is different. Just because a squirrel can eat a certain mushroom or plant doesn't mean that the plant won't harm a human.

SPOTLIGHTING SENSES

What's Happening

Give each student a copy of "Spotlighting Senses." (Fig. 1.1 on page 3.) Read the What's Happening section with your students. Encourage students to begin thinking about senses by asking questions such as "What do you do with your eyes?" "What do you use to find out how a bird sounds?" "Which sense tells you if something is rough or smooth?"

Before moving on to Schoolyard Challenge, build a foundation for this unit:

- Do any of the activities in the Activities section. These activities work well with students of all ages.

- Read or research with your students about senses. A few resources are included to get you started.

- Try Rhonda's Word Play. Each word play is challenging for students and is related to the topic in the unit.

Activities for Presenting Senses

- Have a student stand with his or her back to the rest of the group. Have a classmate say in a natural voice, "Who am I?" and ask the first student to guess who it is by identifying the voice.

- Using jars or plastic cups, set up the following pairs: salt and granulated sugar; cinnamon sugar and powdered chocolate mixed with sugar; baking powder and powdered sugar; and Kool-Aid and vinegar with food coloring to match the Kool-Aid color. Using each pair separately, let the students guess what the cups contain and whether the pair of cups contain the same thing. Ask how they can find out if they can't be sure just by looking.

- Get two or three fruit juices of similar color. Have students hold their noses while they take a taste of each and swallow. Ask if they can guess which juice is which. Repeat the experiment, but this time, after they swallow, have them release their noses. Ask the students if it made any difference.

- Get an empty spray bottle and fill it with water. Add a few drops of old perfume or cologne—enough so you can smell the odor. Have one person run and hide while everyone else closes their eyes and counts to 20. The runner must spray or squirt the path every time he or she takes a few steps. Everyone tracks the runner by following the scent trail.

- Place several objects in a bag. Put a matching set of objects on a tray. Have each student try to find the match to an object on the tray just by feel. You can also have two bags containing matching sets of objects. Each student puts one hand in each bag and tries to pull out the same object from each bag.

- Have the students color two 3" squares of cardboard or paper in any manner they choose. Then have them try to "hide" the cards in plain sight, by matching the colors or pattern to a place. The only rule is that the card MUST show. The class can be divided into two teams, with each team having a specific hiding area (indoor or outdoors). The teams can then switch areas and hunt for the cards.

- Lay a string across the ground. Ask students to see how many animals they can find as they walk along the string.

NATURE AT YOUR DOORSTEP

Spotlighting Senses

What's Happening

Scientists are people who ask questions such as "What makes the sun hot?" "Why do things fall down but not up?" "How do birds sing?" "Why do frogs lay eggs in water?" Scientists want to learn about the world in as many ways as they can. They use their *senses* of sight, hearing, smell, and touch.

Schoolyard Challenge

Your challenge is to be a scientist. You will learn about nature in your schoolyard by using your senses. Ask yourself some questions about learning with your senses. What senses will I use in my schoolyard today? What can I learn using my ears? What can I discover using my nose?

EXTRA! Rhonda's Word Play

The word "sense" is a homonym with the word "cents" and "scents." That means they sound the same. Can you think of any other "senses" words that have homonyms?

Children's Literature

Brandenberg, Aliki. *My Five Senses.* New York: HarperCollins, 1989.

Machotka, Hana. *Breathtaking Noses.* New York: Morrow, 1992.

Martin, William. *Brown Bear, Brown Bear, What Do You See?* New York: Henry Holt, 1983.

National Wildlife Federation. *What Do Animals See, Hear, Smell, and Feel?* Washington, D.C.: National Wildlife Federation, 1990.

Rhonda's Word Play

Try Rhonda's Word Play. Have students think of homonyms that relate to senses. For example, sense, cents, scents; hear, here; peak, peek; eye, I; see, sea; and nose, knows.

Schoolyard Challenge

Ask students to generate their own questions before you read Schoolyard Challenge. After you read Schoolyard Challenge, compare the students' questions to the questions provided. Explain that these are the questions you will begin answering today, and that you will answer the others on another day. Keep the list of questions posted in the classroom so you can add other questions that come up later and check off those that you investigate. Don't worry if you cannot answer the questions the students ask—research them together.

INVESTIGATING

There are many ways to facilitate this investigation. We have found two methods that work well. You can collect data using all the senses in one day, or you can focus on one sense per day, depending on how much time you want to spend on this unit and the age of the students. If you focus on one sense, you may first want to try some of the activities suggested earlier to help students better understand that particular sense, then have them collect data on their Investigation sheet.

In either case, as you walk, guide the students through each sense individually by asking questions such as: What do we see? What can we hear? What can we touch? What can we smell? Students can observe, listen to, touch, and smell their environment. Try to avoid using the word "see" when you don't specifically mean "see." Use "find," "discover," "learn," or other similar words.

As the students get used to identifying the sensations and which sense they are using, you can pick one object to focus on with a number of senses. For example, find a nut. Look at all its colors (lots of different browns, black perhaps, maybe beige or yellow or green); feel its texture and whether it is hard or soft, wet or dry; shake it and listen for rattling; smell it. If possible, take one or two items back to the classroom to recap what each person discovered using their senses. For a follow-up activity, have each student bring some natural item from home to explore and examine.

We have left tasting off this data sheet (see fig. 1.2) so that there is no temptation to have students taste plants. Students need to know that tasting plants or anything else without knowing what they are can be harmful to their health. However, you may want students to look at things that other animals eat, such as red berries, herbs, flowers, and bark, and guess why the animal likes to eat them.

After your walk, talk about what the students saw, heard, smelled, and touched. Create an ongoing classroom bulletin board with pictures the students have drawn of their favorite objects in each category. Create a problem-solving opportunity by telling students they can add to the list as they discover new things, but they can only add something not yet listed.

NATURE AT YOUR DOORSTEP

SENSES
INVESTIGATION

Investigator _Norvia Remo_
Date _7/14/96_
Time _1 pm_
Weather _Hot & Sunny_
Study area _Outside in the woody Park_

QUESTION: What can I discover about nature today by using my senses?

HYPOTHESIS: I **think** that:
I will see: _trees, birds, flowers, squirrels, lizards_
I will hear: _criketts, birds, Leaves-wind blow_
I will smell: _Passion vine flower-peppermint, basil flower cinnamon_
I will touch: _wood tree stub-smooth, rough tree flowers_

DATA: Draw or write what you find:

See 👁	Hear 👂	Smell 👃	Touch ✋
mushroom on the tree log, Flowers, squirrels, frogs, Small ting, Fish in water pond, 4 men walking in park bird watching	People talking, birds, automobile passing, ducks, birds flying in the air - hear their feathers, water fall dripping, change pau	Fresh greeny on trees, bark - plant, Flowers-garlic cinnamon mint, etc.	Flowers, passion vine, Lg Rubber plant, Cuban Oregano Flower-look like mustard greens!

CONCLUSION: No sound of owl
I saw: _I'm glad there were No snakes in sight, very few lizards_
I heard: _I was hoping to heard more forest animal Noise_
I smelled: _Tree bark & greeny of a very shadowy woody area._
I touched: _Flowers, tree stubs, million mosquitoes touch me not visible!_
But because this is a small park there was only a selective few!

Fig. 1.2. Sample Data Sheet.

MAKING COMPARISONS

A number of comparisons can be made. Use the Make a Comparison data sheet in the back of this chapter to have students compare their hypotheses to their compiled data or compare two different data sets from different habitats, times of day or year, or types of weather. If students have collected data on their own data sheets, ask them to place the two data sheets next to each other. Have them circle similarities in one color and differences in another and then transfer their results to their comparison worksheet.

The procedure can be done with class-sized lists as well. Have students circle words or pictures on the poster sheets that are the same or different. Ask if they see anything similar on the two data sheets or posters and if they see something on one sheet that is not on the other. Remember to discuss similarities and differences in the variables as well.

CONNECTING MATHEMATICS

Creating a Representation

In this unit, help students create their own representations of the data they collected. The layout provided can be used to make a *tally chart*. As practice, tally students by gender, shirt or sock color, hair color, or eye color.

Analyzing the Data

Follow-up questions provided in the Analyze Your Data section allow students to begin thinking about the data they collected by reviewing their representation. Older students can write their own answers, or you can use these questions for class discussion purposes.

Solving a Problem

Have students draw one thing that they saw, heard, smelled, or touched. Tell them not to show their drawing to anyone. Have a partner, teams, or the whole class ask questions about what they drew. They can only ask questions that can be answered *yes* or *no*. Give the questioner one point for every question asked. If they ask a question that has already been asked, they get two points. If they guess and are wrong, they get three points. The goal is to accumulate the lowest score while identifying the item. Create a chart with the items and the number of points it took to get the correct answer. This will give students a way to see their progress and you a way to enhance their number sense.

CREATING YOUR OWN INVESTIGATION

Have students take home a new data sheet to collect information from their home environments. They now have the chance to create their own scientific study about senses. A sample letter to parents is provided in the Appendix to explain the student's task and to instruct parents about their role in the process.

NATURE AT YOUR DOORSTEP

MATH CONNECTION - SENSES

Can you create a tally chart?
     How many things did you see, hear, smell and touch during your investigation?

My title: _What I found_

Sense	Number of things found
Seeing	卌 ‖
Hearing	卌 ‖
Smelling	‖‖‖ ‖
Touching	卌 ‖

Fig. 1.3. Sample Data Sheet.

EXTENDING

- Go back to the suggested activities, children's literature, or Rhonda's Word Play and try those you have not done, or try them again with a new twist.
- Reuse the Investigation sheet at different locations, at different times of the day or year, or while on a field trip.
- Review the questions that students asked during the unit and make sure they are all answered.
- Have the students assemble a notebook containing all their investigations so they can see their progress as scientists. This will provide a good assessment for both you and the students as well as something that will make everyone feel proud.
- Go to another *Nature at Your Doorstep* unit.

NATURE AT YOUR DOORSTEP

MATH CONNECTION - SENSES

ANALYZE YOUR DATA

How many things did you see? _____7_____

How many things did you hear? _____8_____

How many things did you smell? _____5_____

How many things did you touch? _____7_____

Which sense did you use the most? __hearing__

Why do you think you used it the most? __Lots of sounds__

_____

Which sense did you use the least? __smell__

Why do you think you used it the least? __I had to choose__

__things to smell__

Draw your favorite find:

mushroom on the log

Fig. 1.4. Sample Data Sheet.

NATURE AT YOUR DOORSTEP
SENSES
INVESTIGATION

Investigator _____
Date _____
Time _____
Weather _____
Study area _____

QUESTION: What can I discover about nature today by using my senses?

HYPOTHESIS: I **think** that:

I will see: _____
I will hear: _____
I will smell: _____
I will touch: _____

DATA: *Draw or write what you find:*

See 👁	Hear 👂	Smell 👃	Touch ✋

CONCLUSION:

I saw: _____
I heard: _____
I smelled: _____
I touched: _____

NATURE AT YOUR DOORSTEP
SENSES
INVESTIGATION

Investigators_____
Date _____
Time _____
Weather _____
Study area _____

QUESTION: What can we discover about nature today by using our senses?

HYPOTHESIS: We **think** that:

we will see: _____
we will hear: _____
we will smell: _____
we will touch: _____

DATA:

See 👁	Hear 👂	Smell 👃	Touch ✋

CONCLUSION:

We saw: _____
We heard: _____
We smelled: _____
We touched: _____

NATURE AT YOUR DOORSTEP
MAKE A COMPARISON

My comparison is between _____

_____

_____

What is the same? *(Write a sentence or draw a picture.)*

What is different? *(Write a sentence or draw a picture.)*

NATURE AT YOUR DOORSTEP
MATH CONNECTION - SENSES

Can you create a tally chart?

How many things did you see, hear, smell, and touch during your investigation?

Title: _____

Sense	Number of things found
Seeing	
Hearing	
Smelling	
Touching	

NATURE AT YOUR DOORSTEP
MATH CONNECTION - SENSES

ANALYZE YOUR DATA

Look at the tally chart you made for your senses data. Answer the following questions:

How many things did you see? _____

How many things did you hear? _____

How many things did you smell? _____

How many things did you touch? _____

Which sense did you use the most? _____

Why do you think you used it the most? _____

_____

_____

Which sense did you use the least? _____

Why do you think you used it the least? _____

_____

_____

Draw your favorite find:

NATURE AT YOUR DOORSTEP

CREATE YOUR OWN

(Title) _____

INVESTIGATION

Investigator _____
Date _____
Time _____
Weather _____
Study area _____

QUESTION: *(What question do you have?)* _____

_____

HYPOTHESIS: *(What is your hyphothesis?)* _____

_____

DATA: *(How will you keep track of your data?)* Create your own data table:

CONCLUSION: I found _____

_____

UNIT 2

TREES

FOCUS

Students develop an awareness and appreciation for similarities and differences among trees. They determine the general form of the tree—leaves, bark, and other features—and distinguish it from other trees.

BACKGROUND INFORMATION

Trees are woody plants that have single trunks at least four inches in diameter and that are usually 10 feet tall or more at maturity. Shrubs have several trunks and are generally smaller. These are general definitions; there are many exceptions. For example, there are mature 40-year-old oak trees in the sand hills of Monahans, Texas, that are 12 inches tall! However, if it looks like a tree to you, it probably is.

Trees have several important parts that can help to distinguish different species.

Leaves come in a wide variety of shapes, sizes, and textures. The various shapes benefit the plants in their chosen habitats. Dry country plants usually have hard, thick leaves to help them hold on to the limited supply of water. Trees in the rain forest have leaves that are smooth and sharply pointed on the tip to help them shed water so they will not become breeding grounds for molds. Fir trees in northern states have needles to limit their exposure to cold, drying winds; the needles are short so they do not become too heavy with snow.

Leaves are the food factory of the plant and contain the substance that makes a plant green: chlorophyll. Trees present their chlorophyll-filled leaves to the sun in distinctive ways, all designed to maximize the energy they soak up. This creates a distinctive *tree shape*. These various shapes are referred to as "crown shapes."

Bark comes in varying thicknesses, textures, and colors, and contains chemicals to protect the tree's circulatory system. A tree's circulatory system moves water from the roots to the branches and leaves, and sugar produced in the leaves to the rest of the tree.

In temperate climates, trees grow during the summer and become dormant in the winter. Each year's growth can be seen, separated from the previous year's growth by a row of tiny holes. Consequently, we can take a cross-section of tree trunk and count the resultant rings inside to determine a tree's age.

Most trees reproduce using *seeds*. These are produced by *flowers* that have been pollinated by the wind, insects, or birds. The resulting seed might be a nut, a bean, or other type of seed and is often hidden within a fruit. Depending on the time of year that you study trees, you may find buds, flowers, or fruits and nuts.

When the students study trees, they only see about half the tree. The other half, the *root system,* is under the ground. Roots pick up water and minerals for the leaves and anchor the tree against wind and other things that might move it from its place in the sun.

TREKKING AROUND TREES

What's Happening

Give each student a copy of "Trekking Around Trees." (Fig. 2.1 on page 17.) Read the What's Happening section of figure 2.1 with your students. Encourage students to begin thinking about trees by asking questions such as "Are trees alive?" "Where do trees come from?" "Have you ever planted a tree?" "Are trees living or not living?" "If you had a tree, what kinds of things would it need to live?" This activity will give you insight into the perceptions students have about trees.

Before moving on to Schoolyard Challenge, continue by building a foundation for this unit:

- Do any of the following activities. These activities work well with students of all ages.

- Read or research with your students about trees. We have included a few resources to get you started.

- Try Rhonda's Word Play. Each word play is challenging for students and is related to the topic in the unit.

Activities for Presenting Trees

- Have students act out the life cycle of a tree: a seed (curl in a ball), a sprout (raise one arm), a sapling (raise two arms and wiggle fingers for leaves), a mature tree (stand tall, arms out, feet spread apart, wiggle your toes for roots, get hit by lightning, become home for wildlife), a dead tree (woodpeckers are knocking), a rotting log with plants and insects (lie down), a new sprout from the rotting wood (raise one arm).

- Introduce students to a new sapling. Examine the bark and roots and scratch the surface to show students the green cambium layer of the tree. Plant the sapling somewhere in your schoolyard.

- Encourage the students to feel the bark of several trees and notice their textures. Ask students to describe how it feels—rough, smooth, scaly, and so forth.

- Examine a cross-section of tree that has been cut down. Ask students if they can identify how old this tree was, when the tree's best growth years were, when the tree had any bad years, and what may have happened to the tree.

Children's Literature

Bash, Barbara. *Ancient Ones: The World of the Old-Growth Douglas Fir.* San Francisco: Sierra Club, 1994.

Coats, Laura Jane. *The Oak Tree.* New York: Macmillan, 1987.

Hiscock, Bruce. *The Big Tree.* New York: Atheneum, 1991.

Thornhill, James. *A Tree in a Forest.* New York: Simon & Schuster, 1991.

Tresselt, Alvin. *The Gift of the Tree.* New York: Lothrop, Lee, & Shepard, 1992.

Trekking Around Trees

What's Happening

Trees are plants. They have *roots* that hold them in the ground and soak up water from the earth. They have a big stem called a *trunk*, and *branches* that have *buds*, *leaves*, *flowers*, or *seeds* on them. The trunk and branches are covered with *bark* the same way that you are covered with skin. Scientists who study trees and other plants are *botanists*.

Schoolyard Challenge

Your challenge is to become a botanist. You will study some of the trees you find. Ask yourself some questions about trees. Do all trees have the same shapes? Do leaves from different kinds of trees look the same or different?

EXTRA! Rhonda's Word Play

It's fun to make word trees. Can you finish the one I've started? Can you make a word tree of your own?

pine

pin

in

Rhonda's Word Play

Students can create word trees with Rhonda. Start with a two-letter word and expand one letter with every new branch. Have a contest to see who can create the tree with the most branches.

Schoolyard Challenge

Read Schoolyard Challenge with your students. Write the questions on the board or on separate chart paper for later use. Add other questions the students have about trees. Explain that the questions in Schoolyard Challenge are the questions you will begin answering today, and that you will answer the others on another day. Keep the list of questions posted in the classroom so you can add ones that come up later and check off those that you investigate. Don't worry if you cannot answer the questions the students ask—research them together.

INVESTIGATING

This unit has two Investigation sheets. Depending on the level and experience of your students (see figs. 2.2, 2.3, and 2.4), choose the one that is most appropriate for your class, or start with Investigation 1 and do Investigation 2 as your students progress.

Investigation 1

You need at least two different kinds of trees for this study. In section 1, get far enough away from the trees to discern their overall shape. It is often helpful to draw the tree in the air with a finger or crayon to determine what basic shape the tree has. Then have your students check off the shape of that tree. You may need to do this several times as a group before the students continue on their own.

Have students find a leaf and look at it, feel it, and smell it. Match it to one of the shapes on the worksheet. Continue doing this until you have a good sample of leaves available. Then look at, touch, and smell the bark.

Have the students make a rubbing of the bark in one of the spaces on the second half of the investigation sheet. Try this on various trees so students can see the differences. Then have the students review their findings. What differences did they find? What differences did they NOT find? How do their investigations compare with their hypotheses?

Investigation 2

Have the students go out in teams of two or more (depending in part on the number of trees available for study). Monitor them as they collect data on their tree. You may want to do one tree as a group to model the data collection process. The first three boxes are identical to the first investigation. After studying the shape, bark, and leaves, have the students look at the pattern of buds on the branch ends if possible. Ask students the following questions: Is there a bud at the tip? Are the buds on the sides directly opposite each other? Are there three or more in a circle? Are they alternating on opposite sides? How big are the buds? What shape are they?

If there are flowers or fruits, have the students investigate them for color, size, shape, texture, and scent. Any additional characteristics the students find can be written in the last data box.

Text continues on page 22.

NATURE AT YOUR DOORSTEP

TREES 1
INVESTIGATION

Investigator _Scott Reynolds_
Date _____
Time _____
Weather _Sunny to Partly cloudy_
Study area _Park_

QUESTION: What kind of trees will I find today?

HYPOTHESES: I **think** that I will find trees with these shapes:

I **think** I will find leaves with these shapes:

I **think** I will find a bark that feels: ☑ rough, ☑ smooth, ☑ bumpy,
☐ _____.

DATA:

Tree shapes: *Fill in one box for each tree that matches the shape picture.*

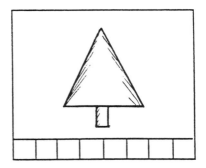
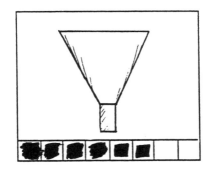
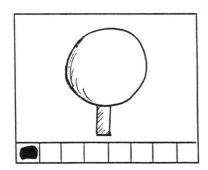

Leaf shapes: *Fill in one box for each tree you find with leaves that match the picture.*

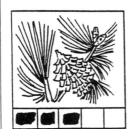

Fig. 2.2. Sample Data Sheet.

NATURE AT YOUR DOORSTEP

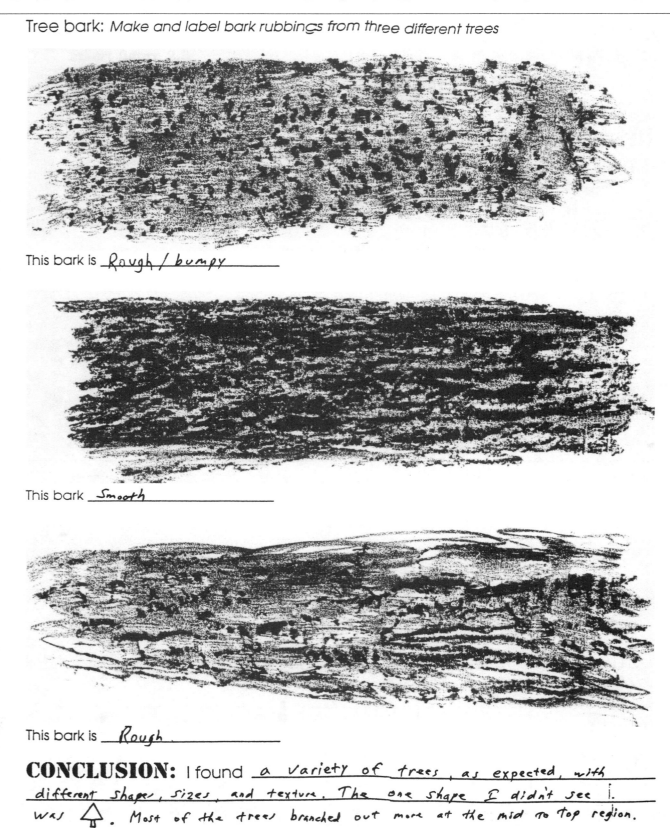

Tree bark: *Make and label bark rubbings from three different trees*

This bark is _Rough / bumpy_

This bark _Smooth_

This bark is _Rough_

CONCLUSION: I found _a variety of trees, as expected, with different shapes, sizes, and texture. The one shape I didn't see. was △. Most of the trees branched out more at the mid to top region._

Fig. 2.3. Sample Data Sheet.

NATURE AT YOUR DOORSTEP

TREES 2
INVESTIGATION

Investigator _Garrick Malone_
Date _5-2-96_
Time _5:40 p m_
Weather _sunny with clouds_
Study area _neighborhood_

QUESTION: What kinds of trees will I find today?

HYPOTHESIS: I **think** that
I will find these shapes: _circle and evergreen_
I will find these leaves: _oaks and pine tree_
I ☑ will ☐ will not find buds.
I ☑ will ☐ will not find flowers or fruits.
I will find _animals in the trees_

DATA: Draw or write what you find:

	Tree #1	comments	Tree #2	comments
Shape	circle tree		Christmas tree shape	
Bark	rough and bumpy		big chunks	
Leaves	oval shape		long, thin and pointy	
Buds	None		None	
Flowers/ Fruits	None		Yes - Pine cones	
Other things	Knots in the trunk		Many dead leaves	
Name	Oak		Pine tree	

CONCLUSION: I found _an oak tree and a pine tree._
Niether one had Birds. Only the pine tree had fruits.

Fig. 2.4. Sample Data Sheet.

As each group completes their initial investigation, have them trade papers and look for the trees described by the other group. This is one way to assess the success of the data collection. The comments section can be used by the second group to state whether the first group's description was helpful.

MAKING COMPARISONS

From the first Investigation sheet, you can compare tree shapes, leaves, and bark. On the second Investigation sheet, students can also compare buds, flowers, or fruits that they find. Also, remember the variables. Comparing trees at different times of the year would be an excellent way to explain growth cycles of trees.

CONNECTING MATHEMATICS

Creating a Representation

For this unit, students can create their own bar graph representations of leaf shapes. (See fig. 2.5.) Depending on the age and experience of the group, you can use the sheet provided or create class-sized graphs. Students will sort and classify leaves they have found in their schoolyard, homes, or neighborhood by leaf shape (leaves could be from trees or shrubs). They should begin by drawing each leaf shape across the bottom of the horizontal axis of the graph. Then they can use any icon (e.g., an X, a check, filling in the whole box) they want to represent the number they collected.

Students can also draw bar graphs to analyze their information by other criteria, as shown in figure 2.6.

Analyzing the Data

Follow-up questions provided in the Analyze Your Data section allow students to think about the data they collected by reviewing their representation. Older students can write their own answers, or you can use these questions for discussion purposes.

Solving a Problem

Have students try this nonroutine problem. You might suggest that they create a table or chart to keep track of all the information. "I have two different kinds of bark (rough and smooth), three different shaped trees (triangular, oval, and round), and four different types of leaves (long and skinny, five-pointed, toothed, and waxy). How many different trees could I build?" (24)

CREATING YOUR OWN INVESTIGATION

This activity is an opportunity for students to take home a new data sheet for making a scientific study about trees in their home environment. A sample letter to parents is provided in the Appendix to explain the student's task and instruct parents about their role in the process.

NATURE AT YOUR DOORSTEP

MATH CONNECTION - TREES

Can you create a vertical bar graph for your data?
Sort your leaves by the shapes at the bottom of the graph.

Title: _Leaf Catagorizing_

number of leaves

leaf shapes

ANALYZE YOUR DATA

Which leaf shape did you find the most? _____

Which leaf shape did you find the least? _____

Why? _Most of the trees contained three lobed leaves_

Fig. 2.5. Sample Data Sheet.

NATURE AT YOUR DOORSTEP

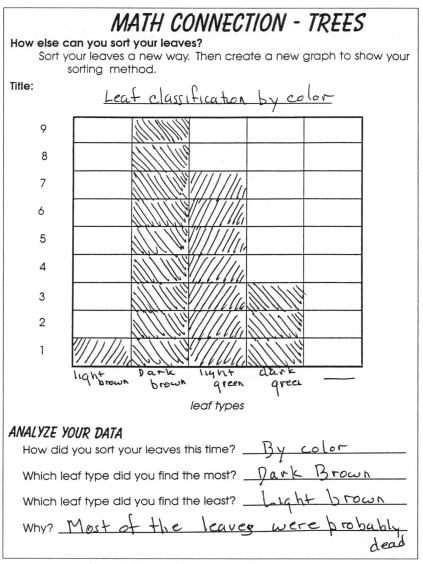

Fig. 2.6. Sample Data Sheet.

EXTENDING

- Go back to the suggested activities, children's literature, or Rhonda's Word Play and try those that you skipped, or try them again with a new twist.

- Reuse an Investigation sheet at different locations, at different times of the day or year, or while on a field trip.

- Review the questions students had during the unit and make sure they are all answered.

- Have the students assemble a notebook containing all their investigations so they can see their progress as scientists. This will provide a good assessment for you and the students as well as something that will make everyone feel proud.

- Go to another *Nature at Your Doorstep* unit.

NATURE AT YOUR DOORSTEP
TREES 1

INVESTIGATION

Investigator _____
Date _____
Time _____
Weather _____
Study area _____

QUESTION: What kind of trees will I find today?

HYPOTHESES: I **think** that I will find trees with these shapes:

I **think** I will find leaves with these shapes:

I **think** I will find a bark that feels: ❑ rough, ❑ smooth, ❑ bumpy,
❑ _____ .

DATA:

Tree shapes: *Fill in one box for each tree that matches the shape picture.*

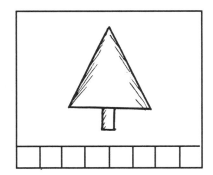 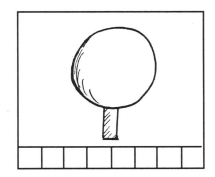 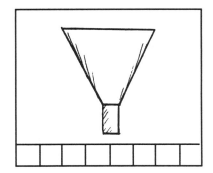

Leaf shapes: *Fill in one box for each tree you find with leaves that match the picture.*

  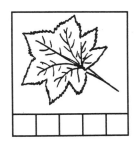  

NATURE AT YOUR DOORSTEP

Tree bark: *Make and label bark rubbings from three different trees.*

This bark is _____

This bark is_____

This bark is _____

CONCLUSION: I found _____

_____

NATURE AT YOUR DOORSTEP
TREES 2
INVESTIGATION

Investigator _____
Date _____
Time _____
Weather _____
Study area _____

QUESTION: What kinds of trees will I find today?

HYPOTHESIS: I **think** that

I will find these shapes:_____
I will find these leaves: _____
I ☐ will   ☐ will not find buds.
I ☐ will   ☐ will not find flowers or fruits.
I will find _____

DATA: Draw or write what you find:

	Tree #1	comments	Tree #2	comments
Shape				
Bark				
Leaves				
Buds				
Flowers/ Fruits				
Other things				
Name				

CONCLUSION: I found _____

_____

NATURE AT YOUR DOORSTEP
MAKE A COMPARISON

My comparison is between _____

_____

_____

What is the same? (*Write a sentence or draw a picture.*)

What is different? (*Write a sentence or draw a picture.*)

MATH CONNECTION - TREES

Can you create a vertical bar graph for your data?
Sort your leaves by the shapes at the bottom of the graph.

Title:

_____

number of leaves

9			
8			
7			
6			
5			
4			
3			
2			
1			

ANALYZE YOUR DATA

Which leaf shape did you find the most? _____

Which leaf shape did you find the least? _____

Why? _____

NATURE AT YOUR DOORSTEP
MATH CONNECTION - TREES

How else can you sort your leaves?

Sort your leaves a new way. Then create a new graph to show your sorting method.

Title:

_____

9				
8				
7				
6				
5				
4				
3				
2				
1				

leaf types

ANALYZE YOUR DATA

How did you sort your leaves this time? _____

Which leaf type did you find the most? _____

Which leaf type did you find the least? _____

Why? _____

NATURE AT YOUR DOORSTEP

CREATE YOUR OWN

Investigator _____
Date _____
Time _____
Weather _____
Study area _____

(Title) _____

INVESTIGATION

QUESTION: *(What question do you have?)* _____

_____

HYPOTHESIS: *(What is your hyphothesis?)* _____

_____

DATA: *(How will you keep track of your data?)* Create your own data table:

CONCLUSION: I found _____

UNIT 3

BIRDS

FOCUS

In this study, students distinguish birds by color, location, and behavior. They begin to recognize that birds are active members of the environment and that they are very adaptable to their surroundings.

BACKGROUND INFORMATION

Ornithology is the study of birds. Birds are among nature's most beautiful and interesting creations. Birds are perfect for people to study because of several traits they share with humans. They rely more heavily on sight than sound to tell them about their environment, they communicate by visual displays and sounds, and they tend to be active during the daytime.

One of the most common ways to tell birds apart is by their color and *field marks*. Field marks are distinguishing features such as crests, eye rings, and wing bars; these marks can be used to separate bird species. The primary color of a bird is generally agreed to be the predominant color of the back, head, and wings rather than that of the belly.

Most birds have numerous features especially designed for flight. First are feathers, which are what distinguish birds from all other animals. They are the ultimate adaptation to flight, as they contour the body, making the bird aerodynamic. In addition, hollow bones and body air sacs make birds very light. Beaks and legs are also designed for flight. Beaks substitute for heavy teeth, further decreasing the bird's overall weight. Bird legs are designed to spring the bird into the air. Birds actually walk on their toes with their knees bent. Have the students get in this position and see how close they are to springing into the air.

Birds occupy a wide range of habitats on earth, and different birds may be adapted to different parts of one habitat. As they search, the students will note that some birds are usually found on the ground, others in the bushes and trees, and others flying in the air. If there is water nearby, students may also see birds swimming.

The study of animal behavior is *ethology*. Because birds are such good study animals, we use them as our introduction to animal behavior. Birds have a number of behaviors that are easily distinguished. *Preening* is the grooming that a bird does to itself or to its partner. Birds are often seen bathing in dust as well as water, hence the term *dusting*. Birds advertise their location and defend their territory by *singing* or *calling*. Birds *court*, often with head bobs, tail wags, wing motions, or posturing. Postures can include drooped wings, cocked tail, and head held high with beak pointed skyward. The peacock's courting display is one of the most widely recognized symbols in the world.

Feeding, nest building, and *resting* are other obvious behaviors. *Flocking* is such a well-recognized concept that the expression "Birds of a feather flock together" is often used to describe members in a group who behave similarly. *Mobbing* is a less well known behavior. Birds often surround and harass another creature, usually one they consider dangerous to them, such as an owl or snake.

BEGINNING BIRDWATCHING

What's Happening

Give each student a copy of "Beginning Birdwatching." (Fig. 3.1 on page 35.) Read the What's Happening section of figure 3.1 with your students. Encourage them to think about birds by asking questions such as "What's special about birds?" "What do the birds in our schoolyard look like?" "What color are they?" "What do they sound like?" "What do the birds do?" "Where do we see birds?" "What makes a bird a bird?"

Before moving on to Schoolyard Challenge, continue by building a foundation for this unit:

- Do any of the following activities. These activities work well with students of all ages.

- Read or research with your students about birds. We have included a few resources to get you started.

- Try Rhonda's Word Play. Each word play is challenging for students and is related to the topic in the unit.

Activities for Presenting Birds

- Have students write about or draw birds they have seen and tell the class about the color of the bird, where it was, and what it was doing when they saw it.

- Have students look through old magazines to find pictures of birds. Students should cut them out and paste them on construction paper, then give descriptive words that you can attach to the pictures. Students who can write may want to compose a paragraph using their descriptive words.

- Kitchen utensils such as prongs, spatulas, and skewers make great models of bird beaks. Students can try to pick up things like sunflower seeds, grapes, gummy worms, and popcorn with the utensils to demonstrate how birds use their beaks.

- Kid-size wings can be made with cardboard, so students can demonstrate how birds soar, glide, flutter, or hover with their wings.

Children's Literature

Bash, Barbara. *Urban Roosts: Where Birds Nest in the City.* San Francisco: Sierra Club, 1991.

Jounce, Gallimard. *Birds: A First Discovery Book.* New York: Scholastic, 1994.

Lerner, Carol. *Backyard Birds of Winter.* New York: Morrow, 1994.

Ryder, Joanne. *Dancers in the Garden.* San Francisco: Sierra Club, 1992.

Yolen, Jane. *Bird Watch.* New York: Philomel, 1991.

Beginning Birdwatching

What's Happening

Birds are the only animals in the world with *feathers*. They can be big or small, with many colors on their feathers or only one. Some run very fast, some can swim, and most can fly. Scientists who study birds are *ornithologists*. They learn about the colors of different birds, where to look for birds, and the different ways they act.

Schoolyard Challenge

Your challenge is to become an ornithologist. You will keep track of birds that you see. Ask yourself some questions about birds, such as: What is the main color of different birds? Where do birds spend their time? What do birds do?

EXTRA! Rhonda's Word Play

Here are some bird riddles. Can you figure out which bird name answers the riddle? What bird is a sad letter? What must you do before you digest your food? What is another way of saying "crazy"? What bird's name is a country? What are thieves doing?

Rhonda's Word Play

In this unit Rhonda presents some bird riddles. Each question represents a different bird. Examples: What is a sad letter? Blue Jay. What must come before digestion? Swallow. What is crazy? Loon or Cuckoo. What is a country? Turkey. What are thieves doing? Robin. See if your students can make up some of their own with the use of field guides or other books about birds.

Schoolyard Challenge

Read Schoolyard Challenge with your students. Write the questions on the board or on separate chart paper for later use. Add other questions the students have about birds. Explain that the questions in Schoolyard Challenge are the questions you will begin answering today, and that you will answer the others on another day. Keep the list of questions posted in the classroom so you can add any that come up later and check off those that you investigate. Don't worry if you cannot answer the questions the students ask—research them together.

INVESTIGATING

In this unit, we suggest starting with Investigation 1 and then moving to either Investigation 2 or 3. The first one is concerned with finding and identifying birds by location. The second focuses on color and the third on behavior. All data sheets ask students to check the appropriate box based on what they see. (See figs. 3.2, 3.3, and 3.4.) Start by having the students fill in their variables and hypotheses.

Birds are often more than one color. As you find birds, allow each student to choose which color they think is the primary one. Blue would probably be the primary color for blue jays, but some students might choose black or white. Encourage the students to approach a bird slowly to get a good look at its colors. They also have the option of reporting that they "can't tell" what color a bird is. This may happen if a student sees only a silhouette or if the bird is too far away to identify.

After collecting data, have the students write their conclusions. Then compare their conclusions with their hypotheses and ask: Were their conclusions the same or different from their hypotheses? Why?

MAKING COMPARISONS

A number of comparisons can be made. Use this worksheet to compare the birds found in the front of the school to the birds found in the back of the school, birds found on bird feeders and birds found in trees, or birds found at different times of the year.

CONNECTING MATHEMATICS

Creating a Representation

For this unit, students can create their own horizontal bar graphs representing the data they have collected about the location of the birds they saw (see fig. 3.5) or what the birds were doing (see fig. 3.6). Depending on the age and experience of the group, you can use the sheet provided or create class-sized graphs. Have students shade in the boxes that correspond to the number of birds they saw in a particular location. Students can create their own graphs to show different locations, colors, or behaviors.

Text continues on page 42.

NATURE AT YOUR DOORSTEP

BIRDS 1

INVESTIGATION

Investigator _Karri_
Date _7/14_
Time _2:35_
Weather _sunny_
Study area _____

QUESTION: Where will I find most birds today?

HYPOTHESIS: I think that I will find most birds _low in bushes_ .

DATA: *Fill in one box for each bird you see.*

In the air :

High in the trees:

Low in the bushes:

On the ground:

CONCLUSION: I found _there to be just a little more birds_ _flying than the ones on the ground_

Fig. 3.2. Sample Data Sheet.

NATURE AT YOUR DOORSTEP

BIRDS 2

INVESTIGATION

Investigator __Karri__
Date __7/14__
Time __1:30__
Weather __Sunny__
Study area __Friends of Bellaire Park__

QUESTION: What color will most birds be today?

HYPOTHESIS: I think that most birds will be __Black__.

DATA: *Fill in one bubble for each bird of that color found.*

☒	Red	○○○○○○○○○○ ○○○○○○○○○○
☐	Orange	○○○○○○○○○○ ○○○○○○○○○○
☐	Yellow	○○○○○○○○○○ ○○○○○○○○○○
☐	Green	○○○○○○○○○○ ○○○○○○○○○○
☒	Blue	●●●●●●●○○○ ○○○○○○○○○○
☐	Purple	○○○○○○○○○○ ○○○○○○○○○○
☐	Brown	●●●●●●●●●● ●●●●●●●●●●
☐	Black	●●●●●●●●●● ●○○○○○○○○○
☐	White	●●●●●●●●●● ●○○○○○○○○○
☐	Gray	●●●●●●●●●● ●●●●●●○○○○
☐	Can't Tell	●●●○○○○○○○ ○○○○○○○○○○

CONCLUSION: I found __that most of the birds were small and brown__

Fig. 3.3. Sample Data Sheet.

NATURE AT YOUR DOORSTEP

BIRDS 3

INVESTIGATION

Investigator _Ellen Davis_
Date _5/11/96_
Time _1:15 pm_
Weather _Sunny_
Study area _Park_

QUESTION: What will the birds be doing today?

HYPOTHESIS: I **think** that the birds will be _Feeding_ _____ today.

DATA:

Preening

Bathing/ Dusting

Feeding

Resting

Singing/ Calling

Nest Building

Courting

Flocking

Mobbing

CONCLUSION: I found _that most birds were resting or singing_

Fig. 3.4. Sample Data Sheet.

NATURE AT YOUR DOORSTEP

MATH CONNECTION - BIRDS

Can you create a horizontal bar graph for your data?
Where were the birds?

Title: _Bird Location_

locations

In the air

High in a tree

Low in a bush

On the ground

1 2 3 4 5 6 7 8 9 10

number of birds

17

20

ANALYZE YOUR DATA:

Where did you see the most birds? _On the ground_

Why do you think you saw the most birds there? _They were looking for food_

Where did you see the least birds? _High in the trees_

Why do you think you saw the least birds there? _I don't know_

Fig. 3.5. Sample Data Sheet.

NATURE AT YOUR DOORSTEP

MATH CONNECTION - BIRDS

Can you create a horizontal bar graph for your data?
What were the birds doing?

Title: _____ Birds _____

behavior

	1	2	3	4	5	6	7	8	9	10
preening	✓	✓								
bathing/dusting	✓									
feeding	✓									
resting	✓	✓	✓							
singing/ calling	✓	✓	✓							
nest building										
courting										
flocking										
mobbing										

number of birds

ANALYZE YOUR DATA

What were most birds doing? _Resting & Singing_

Why do you think they were doing that? _It was a warm spring day?_

Fig. 3.6. Sample Data Sheet.

Analyzing the Data

Follow-up questions provided in Analyze Your Data allow students to think about the data they collected by reviewing their representation. Older students can write their own answers, or you can use these questions for discussion purposes.

Solving a Problem

Have students try this problem: "Little Island has a population of 100 birds. The population doubles every five years. What will the population be in 30 years?" Calculators will be helpful. (In 30 years there will be 6,400 birds; in 60 years there will be 409,600 birds, and in 100 years there will be 104,857,600 birds.)

CREATING YOUR OWN INVESTIGATION

This is an opportunity for students to take home a new data sheet to create their own scientific study about birds and collect information from their home environment. A sample letter to parents is provided in the Appendix to explain the student's task and instruct the parents about their role in the process.

EXTENDING

- Go back to the suggested activities, children's literature, or Rhonda's Word Play and try those you skipped, or try them again with a new twist.

- Reuse an Investigation sheet at different locations, at different times of the day or year, or while on a field trip.

- Review the questions students had during the unit and make sure they are all answered.

- Have the students assemble a notebook containing all their investigations so they can see their progress as scientists. This will provide a good assessment for both you and the students, as well as something that will make everyone feel proud.

- Go to another *Nature at Your Doorstep* unit.

NATURE AT YOUR DOORSTEP
BIRDS 1
INVESTIGATION

Investigator _____
Date _____
Time _____
Weather _____
Study area _____

QUESTION: Where will I find most birds today?

HYPOTHESIS: I **think** that I will find most birds _____.

DATA: *Fill in one box for each bird found in the pictured location.*

In the air:

☐☐☐☐☐☐☐☐☐
　☐☐☐☐☐☐☐☐☐
　　☐☐☐☐☐☐☐☐☐
_____

High in the trees:

☐☐☐☐☐☐☐☐☐
　☐☐☐☐☐☐☐☐☐
　　☐☐☐☐☐☐☐☐☐
_____

Low in the bushes:

☐☐☐☐☐☐☐☐☐
　☐☐☐☐☐☐☐☐☐
　　☐☐☐☐☐☐☐☐☐
_____

On the ground:

☐☐☐☐☐☐☐☐☐
　☐☐☐☐☐☐☐☐☐
　　☐☐☐☐☐☐☐☐☐

CONCLUSION: I found _____

_____

NATURE AT YOUR DOORSTEP
BIRDS 2
INVESTIGATION

Investigator _____
Date _____
Time _____
Weather _____
Study area _____

QUESTION: What color will most birds be today?

HYPOTHESIS: I **think** that most birds will be _____.

DATA: Fill in one bubble for each bird of that color found.

☐ Red   OOOOOOOOO OOOOOOOOO
☐ Orange   OOOOOOOOO OOOOOOOOO
☐ Yellow   OOOOOOOOO OOOOOOOOO
☐ Green   OOOOOOOOO OOOOOOOOO
☐ Blue   OOOOOOOOO OOOOOOOOO
☐ Purple   OOOOOOOOO OOOOOOOOO
☐ Brown   OOOOOOOOO OOOOOOOOO
☐ Black   OOOOOOOOO OOOOOOOOO
☐ White   OOOOOOOOO OOOOOOOOO
☐ Gray   OOOOOOOOO OOOOOOOOO
☐ Can't Tell OOOOOOOOO OOOOOOOOO

CONCLUSION: I found _____

NATURE AT YOUR DOORSTEP
BIRDS 3
INVESTIGATION

Investigator _____
Date _____
Time _____
Weather _____
Study area _____

QUESTION: What will the birds be doing today?

HYPOTHESIS: I **think** that the birds will be _____
_____ today.

DATA:

Preening
○○○○○○○○○○○○○

Bathing/ Dusting
○○○○○○○○○○○○○

Feeding
○○○○○○○○○○○○○○

Resting
○○○○○○○○○○○○○

Singing/ Calling
○○○○○○○○○○○○○○

Nest Building
○○○○○○○○○○○○○○

Courting
○○○○○○○○○○○○○

Flocking
○○○○○○○○○○○○○

Mobbing
○○○○○○○○○○○○○

CONCLUSION: I found _____
_____

NATURE AT YOUR DOORSTEP
MAKE A COMPARISON

My comparison is between _____

_____

_____

What is the same? (*Write a sentence or draw a picture.*)

What is different? (*Write a sentence or draw a picture.*)

NATURE AT YOUR DOORSTEP
MATH CONNECTION - BIRDS

Can you create a horizontal bar graph for your data?
Where were the birds?

Title:_____

locations

In the air

High in a tree

Low in a bush

On the ground

1   2   3   4   5   6   7   8   9   10
number of birds

ANALYZE YOUR DATA:

Where did you see the most birds? _____

Why do you think you saw the most birds there? _____

Where did you see the least birds? _____

Why do you think you saw the least birds there? _____

NATURE AT YOUR DOORSTEP
MATH CONNECTION - BIRDS

Can you create a horizontal bar graph for your data?
What were the birds doing?

Title: _____

behavior

preening										
bathing/dusting										
feeding										
resting										
singing/ calling										
nest building										
courting										
flocking										
mobbing										

1   2   3   4   5   6   7   8   9   10

number of birds

ANALYZE YOUR DATA

What were most birds doing? _____

Why do you think they were doing that? _____

_____

NATURE AT YOUR DOORSTEP

CREATE YOUR OWN

Investigator _____

Date _____

(Title) _____

Time _____

Weather _____

INVESTIGATION

Study area _____

QUESTION: *(What question do you have?)* _____

_____

HYPOTHESIS: *(What is your hyphothesis?)* _____

_____

DATA: *(How will you keep track of your data?)* Create your own data table:

CONCLUSION: I found _____

UNIT 4

INSECTS AND NEIGHBORS

FOCUS

Close observation enables students to differentiate insects and other small animals (insect neighbors) by specific characteristics, such as the number of legs, body parts, or wings each animal has. Students develop knowledge of what insects are (and are not) and that insects are found wherever they look for them.

BACKGROUND INFORMATION

Insects are the most numerous and diverse of all animals that we can see unaided. There are more than 900,000 species of insects—three times more than all other nonmicroscopic animals combined. They occur in virtually every habitat on Earth, from hot springs to snowcapped peaks, from deserts to rain forests. There are even water striders in the middle of the Atlantic Ocean in the Sargasso Sea.

Insects are an excellent study animal for almost any area of biological investigation. To begin to appreciate insects you will want to first recognize one. Insects are members of the jointed-leg phylum Arthropoda. They possess an external skeleton composed of chitin (the hard outer covering); three main body segments (the head, thorax, and abdomen); six legs connected to the thorax; usually four wings (occasionally two or none); and antennae that may be so small as to be almost invisible, or so large they look like bird feathers stuck on the insect's head.

A typical schoolyard has more than a million individual insects of more than a thousand species, so finding them should not be a problem.

INVESTIGATING INSECTS

What's Happening

Give each student a copy of "Investigating Insects." (Fig. 4.1 on page 52.) Read the What's Happening section of figure 4.1 with your students. Once students have started to think about insects, you can introduce them to the investigation. Discuss what students may already know about insects. Ask questions such as "What kinds of insects will we find?" "What kinds of insect neighbors do you think we will find?" "How will we know a creature is an insect?" "How will we know a creature is not an insect?"

NATURE AT YOUR DOORSTEP

Investigating Insects

What's Happening

What has six legs, three main body parts, and antennae? Try looking under a leaf or a log, in flowers, or in the air. Find a small animal that matches this description. You have found an *insect*. If you keep hunting, you will find other animals. Some will be a little different—they may have too many or too few body parts, too many legs, or no antennae. If they don't match the insect description, we can call them *insect neighbors*, because we find them near insects. Scientists who study insects are *entomologists*.

Schoolyard Challenge

Your challenge is to become an entomologist. What kinds of insects and insect neighbors can you find? Ask yourself some questions about insects and insect neighbors. How many kinds of insects can I find? Will I find more insects or neighbors today? How will I know which ones are insects?

EXTRA! Rhonda's Word Play

"As busy as a bee" is a simile about insects. Can you think of other similes?

Before moving on to Schoolyard Challenge, continue by building a foundation for this unit:

- Do any of the following activities. These activities work well with students of all ages.
- Read or research with your students about insects. We have included a few resources to get you started.
- Try Rhonda's Word Play. Each word play is challenging for students and is related to the topic in the unit.

Activities for Presenting Insects and Neighbors

- Have students make an insect out of construction paper or egg cartons and toothpicks. Discuss the basic structure of an insect.
- Watch how insects move and have the students imitate them.
- Have students look at an insect through a hand lens. Ask students to draw their insect, making sure they include all the body parts they can see. Looking at the underside of the insect can be helpful. Then have students look at a spider through a hand lens and draw all of its body parts. Have them compare it to the insect they drew before.
- Put a shovel of dirt on some newspaper, and see how many insects and insect neighbors students can find. As each animal is counted, students can put it back in the hole where the dirt came from. After all creatures are counted, replace the dirt.

Children's Literature

Bernhard, Emery. *Ladybugs*. New York: Holiday House, 1992.

Facklam, Margery. *The Big Bug Book*. New York: Little, Brown, 1994.

Gaffney, Michael. *Secret Forests: A Collection of Hidden Creepy Crawly Bugs and Insects.* New York: Golden Books, 1994.

Heller, Ruth. *How to Hide a Butterfly & Other Insects*. New York: Grosset & Dunlap, 1992.

Wood, Audrey. *Quick as a Cricket*. Singapore: Child's Play (International), 1991.

Rhonda's Word Play

There are familiar similes such as "busy as a bee" or "quick as a cricket." Have students think of other similes for insects or insect neighbors.

Schoolyard Challenge

Read Schoolyard Challenge with your students. Write the questions on the board or on separate chart paper for later use. Add other questions the students have about insects and their neighbors. Explain that you will begin answering the questions in Schoolyard Challenge today, and you will answer the others on another day. Keep the list of questions posted in the classroom so you can add any that come up later and check off those that you investigate. Don't worry if you cannot answer the questions the students ask—research them together.

INVESTIGATING

Begin by reviewing what the students already know about insects: size, structure, habitats, and foods. Make a list of three or four insects with which students are familiar. Ask what kind of place the students think each insect would be found. You will then relate their choices to the sites you have chosen for the investigation. Look through the investigation data sheet with your students, having them write in their variables and hypotheses about which insects will be found at the sites. (See fig. 4.2.) Emphasize that each student can have different predictions. There is no right or wrong answer; each student scientist writes what he or she thinks.

Go to the first site and collect data. Again, each student should fill in the sheet with exactly what that student has seen, not what someone else claims to have seen. Finding no insects is also a valid answer. You may have students work in pairs to help eliminate exaggeration. The students should use all their senses, not just sight, to investigate insects. They should listen to insects and attempt to smell them. It is best not to encourage students to touch insects, unless you know the particular family or species to be harmless. While less than one percent of insects are harmful to humans, common ants, wasps, and some beetles may prove painful if handled. Similar animals like spiders, centipedes, and scorpions may bite or sting.

After the data are collected, have each student or team write a conclusion listing the animals found at each site. Then have them compare their hypotheses with their conclusions. Were they the same or different? Why? (It is just as important when they find what they expected as when they do not.) Repeat this process with the second site. Again compare results and predictions.

MAKING COMPARISONS

Investigate two contrasting sites: perhaps under a log, in the leaf litter, and in bushes or flowers. The students will note that the two areas have different populations of insects and insect neighbors. They can look at the relationships between insects and habitat. What food, shelter, and water does each location (habitat) provide? They can also note the differences and similarities between insects and noninsects that live in the same places.

CONNECTING MATHEMATICS

Creating a Representation

For this unit, students will create their own pictographs of the data they have collected of insects and insect neighbors. Students can create a title for their representation and then draw pictures of each animal in each column, insect or noninsect, to match the data they collected. Continue the process by having students create their own pictographs of winged and nonwinged insects. (See fig. 4.3.)

Analyzing the Data

Follow-up questions provided in this section (see fig. 4.4) allow students to think about the data they have collected by reviewing their representation. Older students can write their own answers, or you can use these questions for discussion purposes.

Text continues on page 58.

NATURE AT YOUR DOORSTEP

INSECTS & NEIGHBORS
INVESTIGATION

Investigator _Ellen Davis_
Date _5/10/96_
Time _11:50_
Weather _Cloudy_
Study area _Park_

QUESTION: What insects and insect neighbors will I find today?

HYPOTHESIS: I **think** that I will find _mosquitos_

DATA: Draw or write the animal and fill in the other information.

Animal	# body parts	# legs	# wings	Insect y/n
Bug	1	6	—	Y
Fly	2	4	2	Y
Black Ant	2	4	—	Y
Ladybug	2	2	2	Y
Bug	1	2	2	Y
Black Bug	2	2	2	Y
Red Ant (long)	3	6	—	Y

CONCLUSION: I found _7 insects) - 3 without_ _wings and 4 with wings._

Fig. 4.2. Sample Data Sheet.

NATURE AT YOUR DOORSTEP

MATH CONNECTION - INSECTS

ANALYZE YOUR DATA

How many winged insects did you see? ___4___

How many wingless insects did you see? ___3___

Which group did you see the most? ___Winged___

Why do you think you saw this group the most? ___easier to locate___

Which group did you see the least? ___Wingless___

Why do you think you saw this group the least? ___difficult to see___

Draw one insect from the winged group with the wings closed or folded.
Are they hard to see? _Yes_

Fig. 4.3. Sample Data Sheet.

NATURE AT YOUR DOORSTEP

MATH CONNECTION - INSECTS

Now see if you can create a pictograph comparing winged and wingless insects that you found.

Title: _Insects_

labels _Winged_   _wingless_

Fig. 4.4. Sample Data Sheet.

Solving a Problem

Have students try this problem: "Jeff collects lizards and beetles. There are 12 creatures in all, with a total of 56 legs. If lizards have four legs and beetles have six legs, how many lizards and beetles does Jeff have?" Making a table might help students solve this problem. (Answer: eight lizards and four beetles.)

CREATING YOUR OWN INVESTIGATION

This is an opportunity for students to create their own scientific study about insects in their home environment. A sample letter to parents is provided in the Appendix to explain the student's task and instruct the parents about their role in the process.

EXTENDING

- Go back to the suggested activities, children's literature, or Rhonda's Word Play and try those you skipped, or try them again with a new twist.

- Reuse the Investigation sheet at different locations, at different times of the day or year, or while on a field trip.

- Review the questions students had during the unit and make sure they are all answered.

- Have the students assemble a notebook containing their investigations so they can see their progress as scientists. This will provide a good assessment for both you and the students, as well as something that will make everyone feel proud.

- Go to another *Nature at Your Doorstep* unit.

NATURE AT YOUR DOORSTEP
INSECTS & NEIGHBORS
INVESTIGATION

Investigator _____
Date _____
Time _____
Weather _____
Study area _____

QUESTION: What insects and insect neighbors will I find today?

HYPOTHESIS: I **think** that I will find _____
_____

DATA: Draw or write the animal and fill in the other information.

Animal	# body parts	#legs	# wings	Insect y/n

59

NATURE AT YOUR DOORSTEP

Animal	# body parts	# legs	# wings	Insect y/n

CONCLUSION: I found _____

_____

_____

_____

NATURE AT YOUR DOORSTEP
MAKE A COMPARISON

My comparison is between _____

_____

_____

What is the same? (_Write a sentence or draw a picture._)

What is different? (_Write a sentence or draw a picture._)

NATURE AT YOUR DOORSTEP
MATH CONNECTION - INSECTS

Can you create a pictograph to compare the number of insects you found to the number of other animals you found?

How many of each group were there?

Title: _____

labels   _____   _____

NATURE AT YOUR DOORSTEP
MATH CONNECTION - INSECTS

ANALYZE YOUR DATA

How many insects did you see? _____

How many insect neighbors did you see? _____

Which group did you see the most? _____

Why do you think you saw this group most? _____

_____

_____

Which group did you see the least? _____

Why do you think you saw this group the least? _____

_____

_____

Draw one insect. Label the parts that helped you identify it.

NATURE AT YOUR DOORSTEP
MATH CONNECTION - INSECTS

Now see if you can create a pictograph comparing winged and wingless insects that you found.

Title: _____

labels   _____   _____

NATURE AT YOUR DOORSTEP
MATH CONNECTION - INSECTS

ANALYZE YOUR DATA

How many winged insects did you see? _____

How many wingless insects did you see? _____

Which group did you see the most? _____

Why do you think you saw this group the most? _____

_____

_____

Which group did you see the least? _____

Why do you think you saw this group the least? _____

_____

_____

Draw one insect from the winged group with the wings closed or folded.
Are they hard to see?

NATURE AT YOUR DOORSTEP

CREATE YOUR OWN

Investigator _____
Date _____
Time _____
Weather _____
Study area _____

(Title) _____

INVESTIGATION

QUESTION: *(What question do you have?)* _____
_____

HYPOTHESIS: *(What is your hyphothesis?)* _____
_____

DATA: *(How will you keep track of your data?)* Create your own data table:

CONCLUSION: I found _____

_____

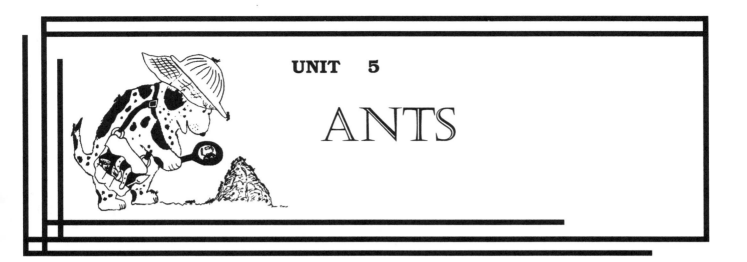

UNIT 5

ANTS

FOCUS

In this study, students experiment with different foods to determine food preferences of ants and then investigate the various behaviors ants exhibit when they encounter one another.

BACKGROUND INFORMATION

Ants can be found on any schoolyard. In most of the southeastern United States, fire ants are common mound builders in schoolyards. They can be excellent experimental subjects, but caution should be exercised because they can inflict a painful sting. Carpenter ants can often be found living in wood structures or dead tree limbs. Pharaoh ants are the tiny "sugar ants" found in houses and along foundation walls inside school buildings.

Ants are social insects and live in colonies that number as few as a dozen individuals to many tens of thousands. A large ant colony is currently referred to by ecologists as being a single "super-organism" because the entire colony functions like a single individual of a higher-order animal. Individual worker ants leave the colony and *forage*—look for food. Ants navigate by visual landmarks or by following scent trails. Ants that use visual landmarks usually follow straight lines to the colony. Those that use scent can take convoluted routes returning to a food supply or colony. By erasing the scent trail, students may observe how ants reestablish the trail, and if they watch very closely they may see ants touch their abdomens to the ground every few steps to make or remark a trail.

To communicate with other members of the colony, ants touch their antennae to the antennae of ants they meet. They also might examine the other ant's entire body with their antennae. The most important communication aspect of ants is the habit of licking one another. In this licking process, called *trophallaxis*, they pass food and chemical messages called *pheromones*.

Foraging workers bring back food for the entire colony, and each member shares its food with almost every ant it meets. This is why poison food baits are very effective controls for individual colonies.

Pheromones are produced by all colony members, but most importantly by the queen. These chemical messages tell the worker ants what they should do and which foods they should gather according to the needs of the colony.

Different types of food fulfill different needs. Protein-rich foods such as cheese, meat, cat food, and eggs are excellent when colonies are rapidly growing and feeding a lot of youngsters in the spring and summer. Sugars provide quick energy and are sought in winter and early spring and after colony disasters such as floods. Complex carbohydrates such as bread are good sustaining foods for summer. Fats, including most oily foods, are not frequently used by ants as they have little ability to digest fat. Some use may be made of fats in the fall.

In the course of their activities, ants frequently encounter ants from other colonies. Their interactions are generally antagonistic and are divided into three categories: *threatening, seizing,* and *dragging.* When threatening, an ant will rear up and open its mandibles. Seizing is literally that, the grabbing of a limb or body part of the other ant. Dragging is also obvious—one ant drags another along the ground. When ants meet at or near food sources (as in these investigations), the patterns of the interactions can change as the numbers of workers from the competing colonies change, an interesting phenomenon to watch.

ANTICIPATING ANTS

What's Happening

Give each student a copy of "Anticipating Ants." (Fig. 5.1 on page 69.) Read the What's Happening section of figure 5.1 with your students. Encourage students to think about ants by asking questions such as "How many ants do you think we will see today? What will they look like?" "Are ants insects? How do you know?" "What do you think ants like to eat? Why?" "What are their distinguishing features?" "How can you tell different species of ants apart?" "How do ants communicate?" "What happens when an ant finds a food supply too big to carry back to the nest by itself?"

Before moving on to Schoolyard Challenge, continue by building a foundation for this unit:

- Do any of the following activities. These activities work well with students of all ages.
- Read or research with your students about ants. We have included a few resources to get you started.
- Try Rhonda's Word Play. Each word play is challenging for students and is related to the topic in the unit.

Activities for Presenting Ants

Take a walk with your students around the schoolyard to find ants. Have them see how many different kinds they can find. If you collect them for later release, be careful not to put more than one species in the same container. Ants can be territorial.

- Have students place an obstacle in the path of an ant and observe how it gets around the obstacle.
- Place a dead fly or other insect in the ant's pathway and have students watch how the ant reacts to it. If it goes for help, notice how one ant communicates with another by means of its antennae.
- Observe ants under a magnifying glass or in a bug box. See if students can locate the eyes, mouth, and antennae. How many segments do the antennae have?
- Buy or build an ant farm to observe metamorphosis and behavior.

Anticipating Ants

What's Happening

Ants are amazing. They live together in colonies in many different kinds of places all over the world. Some ants can lift 50 times their own weight. That's a big help when they need to carry food back to their *colony*. Ants can eat many foods. Scientists who study ants are *myrmocologists*. They learn about the foods ants like and how ants act when they meet each other.

Schoolyard Challenge

Your challenge is to become a myrmocologist. You will find out what kinds of food the ants in your area like. Ask yourself some questions about foods that ants might prefer. Do the ants here like fruits or meats better? Do the ants here like fatty foods?

EXTRA! Rhonda's Word Play

How many words can you think of that have "ant" in them?
Like plANT or assistANT.

Children's Literature

Losito, Linda. *The Ant on the Ground.* London: Belitha, 1989.

Philpot, Lorna, and Graham Philpot. *Amazing Anthony Ant.* New York: Random House, 1993.

Ryder, Joanne. *Under Your Feet.* New York: Macmillan, 1990.

Van Allsburg, Chris. *Two Bad Ants.* Boston: Houghton Mifflin, 1988.

Rhonda's Word Play

Give each student a book about something in nature. Have them find and write as many words as they can that have the word "ant" in them. Keep a class list so you can add words that students find in the future.

Schoolyard Challenge

Read Schoolyard Challenge with your students. Write the questions on the board or on separate chart paper for later use. Add other questions the students have about ants. Explain that you will answer the questions in Schoolyard Challenge today, and you will answer the others on another day. Keep the list of questions posted in the classroom so you can add any that come up later and check off those that you investigate. Don't worry if you cannot answer the questions the students ask—research them together.

INVESTIGATING

Any ant colony is suitable for the investigation. However, colonies are only active when the mound temperature is sufficiently high, so this investigation cannot be done in winter except in extreme southern climates. Depending on the season during which you conduct the study, you will find that the ants exhibit vastly different food preferences, and that as the seasons progress their preferences change. At this point, you may want to go on an ant hunt to find places in your schoolyard where ants are prevalent.

Investigation 1

In this investigation you will be observing the food preferences of ants. (See fig. 5.2.) You will need to set up your experiment an hour or so beforehand. On your own or with the class, choose four foods, each of which would fall primarily in one category: protein (e.g., meat, cheese, eggs); sugar (e.g., white or brown, syrup or honey); fat (e.g., butter, lard, shortening, salad oil); and carbohydrates (e.g., bread, grain, unsweetened cereal). Place the four foods at a site where ants are known to come, and check the site for ants every hour or so.

Review the investigation sheet with the students. Ask them to fill in the food type they think ants will prefer. Then go out to look. Column one is for a description or drawing of the ants. This can be used to identify the ants in a guidebook. In the following four columns, tally the number of ants at each food. The conclusion will record the results of the count.

After you have conducted the investigation and determined what the preference currently is for a colony, you might have the class leave some "natural" foods, like grass seeds, insects, leaves, flowers, and nuts, for the ants and see what they carry off. Then have the students decide what nutrients the natural food is rich in.

NATURE AT YOUR DOORSTEP

ANTS 1
INVESTIGATION

Investigator _Paula_
Date _4-2-96_
Time _1:30 PM_
Weather _warm_
Study area _driveway_

QUESTION: What type of food do ants prefer?

HYPOTHESIS: I **think** that ants will prefer _jam_.

DATA: After _30_ minutes, these ants were found:
90

Ant: draw or describe	food #1 meat	food #2 butter	food #3 bread	food #4 jam	Total
odd tiny 30 red orange 90	8	0	0	0	8
	50	0	0	0	50
odd medium red orange	4	0	$3	3	10
	10	0	0	0	10
black	0	1	1	0	2
	0	0	30	70	100
Total	12 / 60	1 / 0	4 / 30	3 / 70	20 / 160

CONCLUSION: I found _20 ants, 3 kinds - and some fighting_

Fig. 5.2. Sample Data Sheet.

Investigation 2

This is an observation of the interactions among the ants as they go to and from the food. (See fig. 5.3.) The question asks which types of interactions the ants will be engaged in most frequently. The ants involved in the interaction can be drawn or described, and the interaction is identified. Have students match the behavior they observe and the picture on their investigation and check or color in one of the circles. The conclusion sums up the results of the study.

MAKING COMPARISONS

Compare the differences and similarities among the ants you find. Look at the time it takes from the discovery of a food until other ants arrive to help carry it back. Try different foods in the same categories (e.g., fats, carbohydrates, proteins). In addition, study the ants' reaction to disturbing their trails, either by introducing obstacles or by erasing the trails. Compare how different ants react.

CONNECTING MATHEMATICS

Creating a Representation

For this unit, students can create their own line graph representations of the data they have collected about ants to give them a picture of which food the ants liked best. (See fig. 5.4.) Continue the process by having students create their own representations of either the behaviors they observed or the reactions of ants to the obstacles placed in front of them.

Analyzing the Data

Follow-up questions provided in the Analyze Your Data section can be used as a guide for questions about which foods attracted more ants and why. (See fig. 5.5.) These questions also give students another opportunity for hypothesizing why a particular food attracted so many ants and challenge them to test their hypothesis.

Solving a Problem

Three ants—a pharaoh ant, a carpenter ant, and a fire ant—all wanted to try each of the three foods. Can you draw a path from each ant to each food without crossing any lines? (Hint: The problem is solvable if one of the lines crosses a line representing a house. See one possible answer below.)

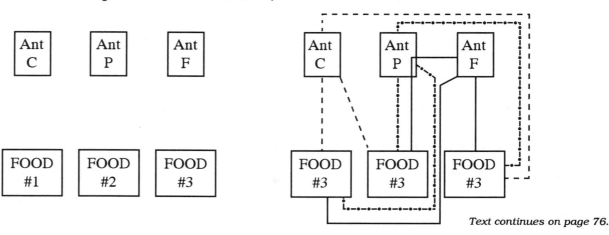

Text continues on page 76.

NATURE AT YOUR DOORSTEP

ANTS 2

INVESTIGATION

Investigator _Ellen G_
Date _4-20-96_
Time _1 pm_
Weather _SUNNY_
Study area _PARKING LOT_

QUESTION: How are the ants behaving today?

HYPOTHESIS: I **think** that ants will be ☑ touching antennae, ☑ examining, ☑ licking, ☑ threatening, ☐ seizing, ☐ dragging.

DATA:

Ants from the same colony

Touching antennae

Examining

Licking

Ants from different colonies

Threatening

Seizing

Dragging

CONCLUSION: I found _MORE ANT FIGHTING THAN FRIENDLY_

Fig. 5.3. Sample Data Sheet.

NATURE AT YOUR DOORSTEP

MATH CONNECTION - ANTS

Can you create a line graph to show how many ants visited each type of food?

Title: *What foods ants like*

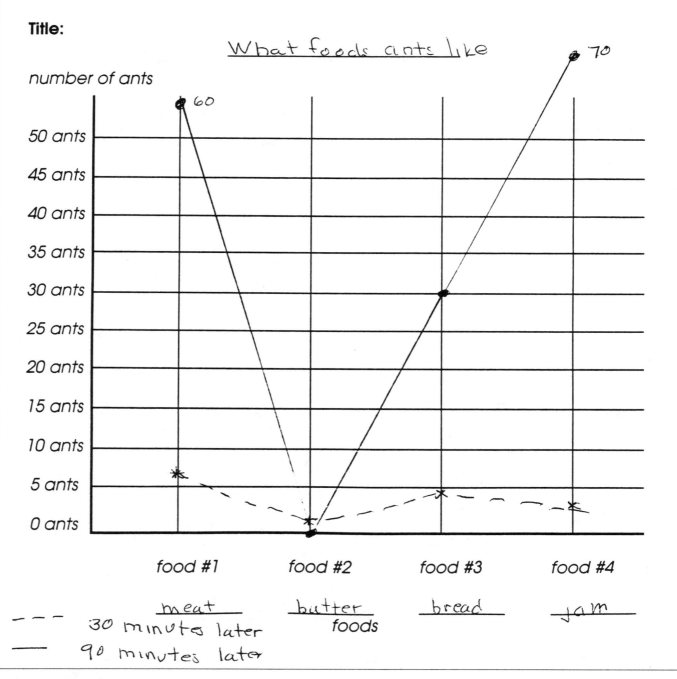

Fig. 5.4. Sample Data Sheet.

NATURE AT YOUR DOORSTEP

MATH CONNECTION - ANTS

ANALYZE YOUR DATA

Which food attracted the most ants? *meat*

Why do you think it attracted the most ants? *It is the best for them. lots of nutrition*

Which food attracted the fewest ants? *butter*

Why do you think it attracted the fewest? *It just has fat*

How could you test your hypotheses? *Feed some ants just fat and see if they die.*

Draw one kind of ant you observed:

black at with bent antenna

Fig. 5.5. Sample Data Sheet.

CREATING YOUR OWN INVESTIGATION

This is an opportunity for students to create their own scientific study about ants in their home environment. A sample letter to parents is provided in the Appendix to explain the student's task and instruct the parents about their role in the process.

EXTENDING

- Go back to the suggested activities, children's literature, or Rhonda's Word Play and try those you skipped, or try them again with a new twist.

- Reuse the Investigation sheet at different locations, at different times of the day or year, or while on a field trip.

- Review the questions students had during the unit and make sure they are all answered.

- Have the students assemble a notebook containing all their investigations so they can see their progress as scientists. This will provide a good assessment for both you and the student, as well as something that will make everyone feel proud.

- Go to another *Nature at Your Doorstep* unit.

NATURE AT YOUR DOORSTEP
ANTS 1
INVESTIGATION

Investigator _____
Date _____
Time _____
Weather _____
Study area _____

QUESTION: What type of food do ants prefer?

HYPOTHESIS: I **think** that ants will prefer _____.

DATA: After _____ minutes, these ants were found:

Ant: draw or describe	food #1	food #2	food #3	food #4	Total
Total					

CONCLUSION: I found _____

NATURE AT YOUR DOORSTEP
ANTS 2
INVESTIGATION

Investigator _____
Date _____
Time _____
Weather _____
Study area _____

QUESTION: How are the ants behaving today?

HYPOTHESIS: I **think** that ants will be ❑ touching antennae, ❑ examining, ❑ licking, ❑ threatening, ❑ seizing, ❑ dragging.

DATA:

Ants from the same colony · Ants from different colonies

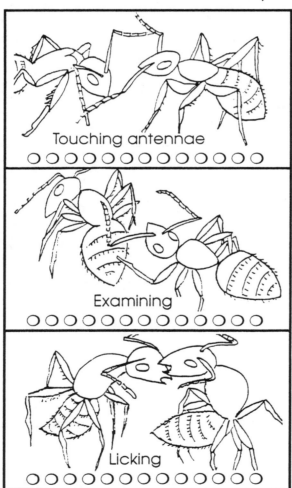

Touching antennae
○○○○○○○○○○○○○○

Examining
○○○○○○○○○○○○○○○

Licking
○○○○○○○○○○○○○○○

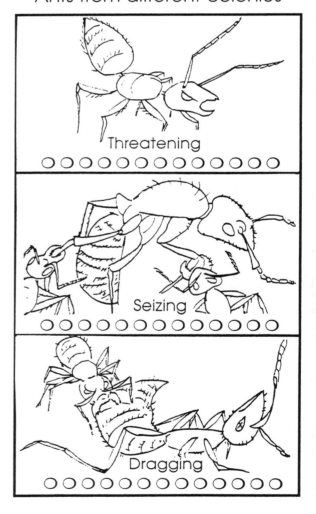

Threatening
○○○○○○○○○○○○○○

Seizing
○○○○○○○○○○○○○○○

Dragging
○○○○○○○○○○○○○○○

CONCLUSION: I found _____

_____

NATURE AT YOUR DOORSTEP
MAKE A COMPARISON

My comparison is between _____

_____

_____

What is the same? (*Write a sentence or draw a picture.*)

What is different? (*Write a sentence or draw a picture.*)

NATURE AT YOUR DOORSTEP
MATH CONNECTION - ANTS

Can you create a line graph to show how many ants visited each type of food?

Title: _____

number of ants

50 ants

45 ants

40 ants

35 ants

30 ants

25 ants

20 ants

15 ants

10 ants

5 ants

0 ants

food #1   food #2   food #3   food #4

_____   _____   _____   _____

foods

NATURE AT YOUR DOORSTEP
MATH CONNECTION - ANTS

ANALYZE YOUR DATA

Which food attracted the most ants?_____

Why do you think it attracted the most ants? _____

_____

_____

Which food attracted the fewest ants?_____

Why do you think it attracted the fewest?_____

_____

_____

How could you test your hypotheses? _____

_____

_____

Draw one kind of ant you observed:

NATURE AT YOUR DOORSTEP

CREATE YOUR OWN

Investigator _____
Date _____
Time _____
Weather _____
Study area _____

(Title) _____

INVESTIGATION

QUESTION: *(What question do you have?)* _____

_____

HYPOTHESIS: *(What is your hyphothesis?)* _____

_____

DATA: *(How will you keep track of your data?)* Create your own data table:

CONCLUSION: I found _____

_____

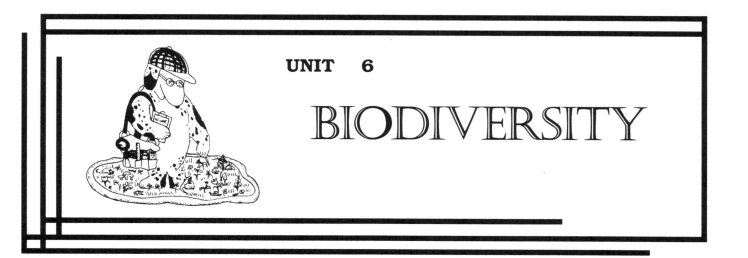

UNIT   6

BIODIVERSITY

FOCUS

This investigation guides students to explore the many kinds of living organisms found in their schoolyard. By looking at different sites, students realize the variety (biodiversity) of plants and animals that exist.

BACKGROUND INFORMATION

Bio—from the Greek word meaning "life." *Diversity*—the condition of being different or of having differences. Biodiversity (short for *biological diversity*) is a convenient label used to refer to the variety and variability of the Earth's life forms. If a wide variety of species lives in an area, the biodiversity is said to be high. If only a few species inhabitant an area, biodiversity is low. The importance of biodiversity is a topic of research currently receiving a lot of attention around the world.

Scientists study several levels of biodiversity. The one primarily involved in this unit is *species diversity*, calculating the number of different types or species of plants, animals, and fungi that inhabit an area. Another level is *genetic diversity*. This refers to the variability of individuals within one species. Differences in height, running ability, foot shape, eye color, and the like are measures of this level of biodiversity. The last major division is *ecosystem diversity*, which measures the diversity of environments themselves. Grasslands, deserts, rain forests, and oceans are examples of the diversity we find at this level.

These different levels of biodiversity are not independent of each other. Different ecosystems make different requirements on the plants and animals that live there, be it adapting to tidal changes along the coast or tolerating long periods without rain in a desert. A range of characteristics among the individuals of a species makes it more likely that some will be able to adapt to changing conditions (e.g., drought, pollution). A wide range of species in an area provides potential substitutes for species that die out, thus preventing a collapse of the whole system.

Biologists who study biodiversity can end up being detectives, researchers, and explorers all rolled into one.

BELIEVING IN BIODIVERSITY

What's Happening

Give each student a copy of "Believing in Biodiversity." (Fig. 6.1 on page 85.) Read the What's Happening section of figure 6.1 with your students. Encourage them to begin thinking about biodiversity by asking questions such as "How many plants and animals do you think live in our schoolyard? Do you think we can see them all?" "How big is the biggest living thing in our schoolyard? The smallest?"

Before moving on to Schoolyard Challenge, continue by building a foundation for this unit:

- Do any of the following activities. These activities work well with students of all ages.

- Read or research with your students about biodiversity. We have included a few resources to get you started.

- Try Rhonda's Word Play. Each word play is challenging for students and is related to the topic in the unit.

Activities for Presenting Biodiversity

- Have students look around the room at their classmates. What differences do they see? Keep a list. The list should include different skin color, eye color, hair color, hair texture, height, hand span, and so on. This demonstrates the diversity of people, whereas biodiversity looks at the diversity of all living things in a particular area.

- Ask students to estimate how many different plants there are in their schoolyard. Then take a walk with your students and collect as many different types of leaves as possible. Discuss how each leaf represents a different type of plant. How close were they to their estimate? Do they think they found every plant? Estimate how many there might be in your city.

Children's Literature

Baker, Jeannie. *Where the Forest Meets the Sea.* New York: Greenwillow, 1988.

Goodman, Susan. *Bats, Bugs, and Biodiversity.* New York: Simon & Schuster, 1995.

Wells, Robert. *What's Smaller Than a Pigmy Shrew?* Morton Grove, IL: Albert Whitman, 1995.

Rhonda's Word Play

See how many words your students can find in the word "biodiversity," such as *dive, bid, divert, sit,* and *driver.* While you are doing this unit, keep a class list of words and see how diverse biodiversity really is.

Believing in Biodiversity

What's Happening

There are millions and millions of kinds of plants and animals in the world. Some places have many different plants and animals living there. Scientists say that those places have a lot of *biological diversity* or *biodiversity*. If a place has only a few kinds of plants and animals, they say it has only a little biodiversity. Scientists agree that a lot of biodiversity in the world is good for all of us. A *biologist* is a scientist who studies different kinds of plants and animals in the world.

Schoolyard Challenge

Your challenge is to become a biologist and figure out how much biodiversity there is in your area. You will count the different kinds of plants and animals in two sites and discover which site has the greatest biodiversity.

EXTRA! Rhonda's Word Play

How many different words can you form with the letters from the word "biodiversity"?

Schoolyard Challenge

Read Schoolyard Challenge with your students. Write the questions on the board or on separate chart paper for later use. Add other questions the students have about biodiversity. Explain that the questions in the *Schoolyard Challenge* are the questions you will begin answering today, and you will answer the others on another day. Keep the list of questions posted in the classroom so you can add any that come up later and check off those that you investigate. Don't worry if you cannot answer the questions the students ask—research them together.

INVESTIGATING

This investigation requires a degree of preparation. Two sites of approximately equal size need to be chosen. They do not need to be large; a 10-foot square is sufficient, and preferable to a whole yard, where small organisms are likely to be overlooked. You may want to mark the chosen areas with cones, stakes, or ribbons. Try to choose two different types of sites, such as a yard and a flower bed or a sidewalk border and a hedge.

On this worksheet, the students will hypothesize which site will have the most different types of organisms. Then they will begin the count. Have them observe the site from a distance to make their hypotheses and to look for any larger animals (e.g., birds, squirrels) that might be frightened off at your approach.

Have each student write down only those organisms which he or she sees. (See fig. 6.2.) Encourage the students to work in pairs, to share their finds, or to confirm each new find with you (or with another adult). This discourages exaggeration and promotes careful observation, especially of various grasses, small weeds, small insects, or spiders.

When you don't know the name of a species, give it a label that includes a descriptive term that will help you remember the plant or animal later. This will prevent you from counting one species two or three times.

Your students may want to collect specimens for further observation or comparison. They need to understand that care must be taken so that animals and plants are not overcollected. If a plant has enough leaves, the group can take one leaf and tape it on a piece of paper or the back of a clipboard. Insects caught in bug catchers should be released in the same place they were caught.

At the end of the species search at each site, have the students total the species found. Depending on the students' math level, you can have them take an average or mean for comparison with the other site. You can also make a group total by having one person from each group read several items off their list, then the next group, then back to the first group, and so on until everyone's lists are exhausted. While one group is naming, the other should be checking things off that they have in common. Rotating allows everyone to name something from the list that they may have found and were excited about.

Note which site had the most variety. Ask the students *why* they think one site has more variety than the other. Would they get the same result at a different time of day or year? Why?

MAKING COMPARISONS

A number of comparisons can be made. Compare the plants at the two sites and compare the animals similarly. Compare proportions of plants and animals at one site or between sites. Also, you may want to place students in pairs and have them compare their data sheet with their partners. Try this activity again at different times of the year or day and compare. If you go on a field trip where there are sites different from your schoolyard, compare that one to your schoolyard sites.

NATURE AT YOUR DOORSTEP

BIODIVERSITY
INVESTIGATION

Investigator __Garrick Malone__
Date __6-6-96__
Time __9:30 am__
Weather __overcast__
Study area __patio (#1) & yard (#2)__

QUESTION: Which site will have the greatest biodiversity?

HYPOTHESIS: I **think** that site # __1__ will have the greatest biodiversity.

DATA: List the species of plants and animals you find.

Site #1 __Patio__

Plant or animal species found	Plant or animal species found
doodle bug	clover
slug	1 leafed plant
bess beetle	3 lobed leaf plant
lady bug	small plant
grasshopper	bushy green plant
ants	
big leafy plant	
red green & yellow leaf plant	
tall, stringy plant	
prickly plant	
red flowering plant	
small green leafy plant	
algae	
cactus	
rough barked tree	
Species count: 15	Species count: 5

Total Species count: __20__

Fig. 6.2. Sample Data Sheet.

CONNECTING MATHEMATICS

Creating a Representation

Students can create their own two-part circle graphs. (See fig. 6.3.) The graphing opportunity presented here is to have students create a circle graph that shows animals versus plants. For younger students, you may want to start by making a large circle with tape or string on the floor and having the students represent the plants and animals. Use additional tape or string to split the difference. If you take two different colored paper plates, cut a slit halfway through each plate and slide them together so you can demonstrate how their circle graph should look. Provide small plates for students so they can match yours and then go back to their desks to draw a graph on their paper.

Cut Plate 1   Cut Plate 2   Plates 1 and 2 together.

Analyzing the Data

Follow-up questions provided in the Analyze Your Data section (see fig. 6.4) can be used as a guide for questions about fractional parts and critical thinking questions. Students can write their own answers, or you can use the questions for discussion purposes.

Solving a Problem

Ask students to think about two or three other things that they could graph using circle graphs. Possibilities might include small plants versus trees or insects versus mammals versus reptiles or amphibians.

CREATING YOUR OWN INVESTIGATION

This is an opportunity for students to create their own scientific study about biodiversity in their home environment. A sample letter to parents is provided in the Appendix to explain the student's task and instruct the parents about their role in the process.

EXTENDING

- Go back to the suggested activities, children's literature, or Rhonda's Word Play and try those you skipped, or try them again with a new twist.

- Reuse the Investigation sheet at different locations, at different times of the day or year, or while on a field trip.

- Review the questions students had during the unit and make sure they are all answered.

- Have the students assemble a notebook containing all their investigations so they can see their progress as scientists. This will provide a good assessment for both you and the student, as well as something that will make everyone feel proud.

- Go to another *Nature at Your Doorstep* unit.

NATURE AT YOUR DOORSTEP

MATH CONNECTION - BIODIVERSITY

Can you create a circle graph from the data you have collected?

How many living things did you find? __20__

How many were animals? __6__

How many were plants? __14__

Which was more, the number of plants or the number of animals?

__Plants__

Title: __Plant and Animal__

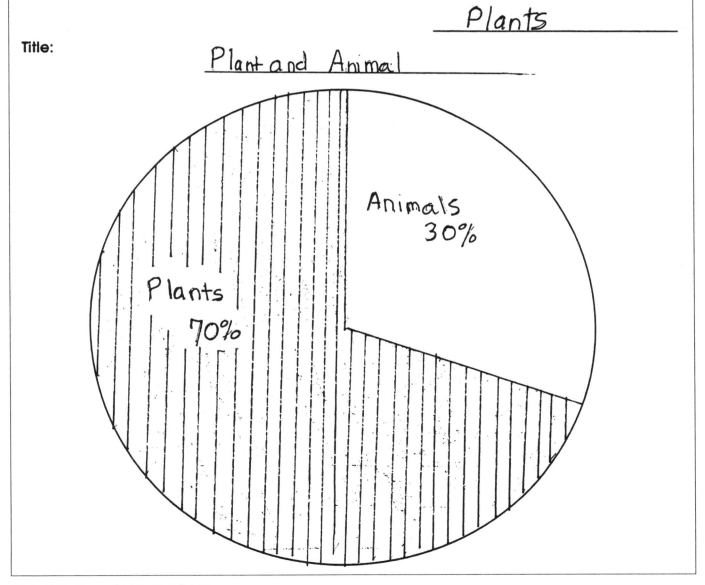

Animals 30%

Plants 70%

Fig. 6.3. Sample Data Sheet.

NATURE AT YOUR DOORSTEP

MATH CONNECTION - BIODIVERSITY

ANALYZE YOUR DATA

Graph title: <u>Plant and Animal</u>

Which section of your graph is bigger? <u>Plant Section</u>

Why do you think it is bigger? <u>There is more diversity</u>
<u>of plants on the patio</u>

Which section is smaller? <u>Animal</u>

Why do you think it is smaller? <u>It is harder to find</u>
<u>all the types of animals because</u>
<u>sometimes they are hiding</u>

Is the smaller section greater than 1/4 or less than 1/4 of the circle?

<u>greater than $\frac{1}{4}$</u>

Is the smaller section greater than 1/3 or less than 1/3 of the circle?

<u>less than 1/3</u>

What other things can you think of that you can chart from your data?

<u>Potted plants + ground plants</u>
<u>Different kinds of animals (reptile.</u>
<u>Insect, etc.)</u>

Fig. 6.4. Sample Data Sheet.

NATURE AT YOUR DOORSTEP
BIODIVERSITY
INVESTIGATION

Investigator _____
Date _____
Time _____
Weather _____
Study area _____

QUESTION: Which site will have the greatest biodiversity?

HYPOTHESIS: I **think** that site # _____ will have the greatest biodiversity.

DATA: List the species of plants and animals you find.

Site #1 _____

Plant or animal species found	Plant or animal species found
Species count:	Species count:

Total Species count: _____

NATURE AT YOUR DOORSTEP

DATA: List the species of plants and animals you find.

Site #2 _____

Plant or animal species found	Plant or animal species found
Species count:	Species count:

Total species count; _____

CONCLUSION: I found _____

_____

_____

_____

_____

NATURE AT YOUR DOORSTEP
MAKE A COMPARISON

My comparison is between _____

_____

_____

What is the same? *(Write a sentence or draw a picture.)*

What is different? *(Write a sentence or draw a picture.)*

NATURE AT YOUR DOORSTEP
MATH CONNECTION - BIODIVERSITY

Can you create a circle graph from the data you have collected?

How many living things did you find? _____

How many were animals? _____

How many were plants? _____

Which was more, the number of plants or the number of animals?

_____

Title:_____

NATURE AT YOUR DOORSTEP
MATH CONNECTION - BIODIVERSITY

ANALYZE YOUR DATA

Graph title: _____

Which section of your graph is bigger? _____

Why do you think it is bigger? _____

_____

_____

Which section is smaller? _____

Why do you think it is smaller? _____

_____

_____

Is the smaller section greater than 1/4 or less than 1/4 of the circle?

_____

Is the smaller section greater than 1/3 or less than 1/3 of the circle?

_____

What other things can you think of that you can chart from your data?

_____

_____

_____

NATURE AT YOUR DOORSTEP

CREATE YOUR OWN

(Title) _____

Investigator _____
Date _____
Time _____
Weather _____
Study area _____

INVESTIGATION

QUESTION: (What question do you have?) _____
_____

HYPOTHESIS: (What is your hyphothesis?) _____
_____

DATA: (How will you keep track of your data?) Create your own data table:

CONCLUSION: I found _____

UNIT 7

HABITATS

FOCUS

In this study, students develop an awareness of what animals need to survive by searching their schoolyard for adequate and appropriate sources of food, water, and shelter for certain animals. Through this exploration, students infer whether their study area can provide a good habitat for these animals.

BACKGROUND INFORMATION

A habitat is a place where specific plants and animals can live successfully. It is defined in *Webster's Dictionary* as "the region where a plant or animal naturally grows or lives; native environment, or place where a person or thing is normally found." It must supply sufficient food, water, space, and shelter and can include the place where the animal builds a home and the supply of materials needed to construct it. Habitat quality can range from excellent to poor depending on the quantity and quality of the food, water, and shelter available for the plant or animal being considered.

The plants and animals that inhabit an area and form the habitat's community are often the food, shelter, and water resources for each other. Some community members, both plants and animals, are food for other members. Some community members, usually (but not always) plants, provide the shelter and building materials for other members. Dew condensing on plants and rain collecting in leaves, bark, or holes can provide water for some animals.

HOMING IN ON HABITATS

What's Happening

Give each student a copy of "Homing in on Habitats." (Fig. 7.1 on page 98.) Read the What's Happening section of figure 7.1 with your students. Encourage students to think about habitats by asking questions such as "What animals could be using our schoolyard as a habitat?" "Where would they find shelter? Food? Water?"

Before moving on to Schoolyard Challenge, continue by building a foundation for this unit:

- Do any of the following activities. These activities work well with students of all ages.

Homing in on Habitats

What's Happening

A *habitat* is a place where something lives. A field can be the habitat for a wildflower and for a field mouse. If the habitat is a good one for an animal, it has enough food, clean water, and places for the animal to find shelter. A good shelter protects the animal from bad weather or provides an escape from enemies. A scientist who studies animals and their habitats is called an *ecologist.*

Schoolyard Challenge

Your challenge is to become a good ecologist. You will look for the right kinds of food, enough water, and good shelters for several animals. Ask yourself some questions about animal habitats. What kinds of food does our schoolyard have? How much water do different animals need?

EXTRA! Rhonda's Word Play

I found a habitat
for a little, tiny bat.
It was a dark, deep cave.
Food, water, shelter it gave.

This is my habitat poem. Can you create a poem about your favorite animal and its habitat?

Fig. 7.1

- Read or research with your students about habitats. We have included a few resources to get you started.

- Try Rhonda's Word Play. Each word play is challenging for students and is related to the topic in the unit.

Activities for Presenting Habitats

- Have the students draw their own habitat. Have them label where they get water, shelter, food, and space.

- Sit in a circle and have students exchange stories about the animals that live in their neighborhood. What have they seen them do? Where do they think they sleep? Where do they think they get their food and water?

- Have students cut their favorite animal out of a magazine and draw what they think that animal's habitat looks like.

Children's Literature

Dunbar, Joyce. *Ten Little Mice.* New York: Harcourt Brace, 1990.

Forsyth, Adrian. *The Architecture of Animals.* Camden East, Ontario: Camden House, 1989.

Hacker, Randy, and Jackie Kaufman. *Habitats: Where the Wild Things Live.* New York: W. W. Norton, 1992.

James, Simon. *The Wild Woods.* Cambridge, MA: Candlewick, 1993.

Kitchen, Bert. *And So They Build.* Cambridge, MA: Candlewick, 1993.

Rhonda's Word Play

Rhonda provides an example of a poem about animals and their habitats. Have your students create another poem about their favorite animal and its habitat.

Schoolyard Challenge

Read Schoolyard Challenge with your students. Write the questions on the board or on separate chart paper for later use. Add any questions the students have about habitats. Explain that the questions in the Schoolyard Challenge are the questions you will begin answering today, and that you will answer the others on another day. Keep the list of questions posted in the classroom so you can add any that come up later and check off those that you investigate. Don't worry if you cannot answer the questions the students ask—research them together.

INVESTIGATING

This investigation can be completed two different ways using the same Investigation sheet. Both work equally well. First you start with a list of animals. You can choose the animals whose habitats you will be looking for and have the students write or draw them in the "animal" column. With older or more experienced students you can let them generate a list of animals from which they each choose seven.

Before you begin the investigation, outline some of the things you might be looking for, such as nuts, berries, or seeds as food; trees or leaves for shelter; and puddles, ponds, or a leaky hose for water. Then go on your walk to see if students can find proper sources for the animals they have selected.

You may want to begin by doing one animal together, as students need to remember that all three components need to be present for a good habitat. For example, if you find acorns, a puddle, and a tree, you might suggest that your schoolyard provides a good habitat for a bird or a squirrel.

Encourage your students to look extra hard for habitat elements for animals they *don't* think can live in the schoolyard. This is a good way to avoid finding only what they expect to find, and a method scientists often use. Once they have made a hypothesis, they try to prove themselves wrong.

The conclusion is a list of the animals for which your students did find food, shelter, and water. (See fig. 7.2.) Your students may find food, shelter, and water needs for animals that do not actually live in the study area. Ask the students why those animals are not found there. What are the other factors involved: noise, traffic, too many people?

MAKING COMPARISONS

Use this sheet to compare habitats of different schoolyard animals or compare the animals found in one habitat (e.g., a rotting log) to the animals found in another habitat (e.g., a live tree). In addition, have students compare their favorite schoolyard animal's habitat to their own habitat.

CONNECTING MATHEMATICS

Creating a Representation

The first part of the habitat math connection provides students with a problem. From the tables, they are to choose the appropriate shelter, drink, food, and amount of land needed to sustain a creature called a Whatsit for one week. Have students look at each table and circle the appropriate items from each store. (See fig. 7.3.)

In this unit, students are asked to represent their information by creating a shopping list using the items they have selected. (See fig. 7.4.) They will need to decide how many of each item they will need for one week, how much these items will cost, and how much the total is. Create a greater challenge by limiting the amount of money the student can spend.

Analyzing the Data

Follow-up questions help the student think through their decisions. Why did they choose that particular food, shelter, water, and space? If you were a Whatsit, would you feel like you were getting a good habitat? Why?

Solving a Problem

Have students draw this picture:

Whatsit *

* Whatsit's Habitat

Text continues on page 104.

NATURE AT YOUR DOORSTEP

HABITAT
INVESTIGATION

Investigator _Alex Malone_
Date _5-2-96_
Time _8:20_
Weather _clear, Humid_
Study area _Front Yard_

QUESTION: Can the study area provide habitats for animals? Which kinds?

HYPOTHESIS: I **think** I will find habitats for these animals: _squirrels_ _birds, ants, worms, mosquito's,_

DATA: Fill in the chart below:

Animal	foods	shelters	water sources
ant	grass, leaves insects	soft moist ground	moist ground puddle
carpenter ant		dead trees	rain
bird	small insects	tall trees	swimming pool
squirrels		trees	puddle
worms	decomposing stuff	dirt	puddle
mosquitos	humans	trees grass	humans

CONCLUSION: I found habitats for these animals in the study area:
ants, birds, squirrels, worms, mosquitos

Fig. 7.2. Sample Data Sheet.

NATURE AT YOUR DOORSTEP

MATH CONNECTION - HABITAT

Can you design a habitat for a Whatsit?

A Whatsit needs a shelter that is 4 inches high, 4 inches wide and 4 inches deep. It eats three insects and two berries every day. It drinks one cup of water a day. It also needs 1 acre of space.

Circle the things that you would buy from each of the stores below to create a good habitat for a Whatsit.

Shelter Store

Item	Price
4" x 4" piece of wood	$0.50 each
Hay	$0.10 per handful
Brick - 4" x 2"	$0.50 each
Roof	$1.00 each

Drink Store

Item	Price
Water	$0.25 per cup
Juice	$0.35 per cup
Milk	$0.10 per cup
Soda	$0.15 per cup

Food Store

Item	Price
Berry	$0.10 each
Leaf	$0.20 each
Apple	$0.35 each
Candy Bar	$0.50 each
Hamburger	$1.00 each
Grasshopper	$0.30 each

Land Store

Item	Price
Square Foot	$2.00 each
Acre	$5.00 each
Square Yard	$3.00 each
Square Inch	$1.00 each

Fig. 7.3. Sample Data Sheet.

NATURE AT YOUR DOORSTEP

MATH CONNECTION - HABITAT

ANALYZE YOUR DATA

Create a habitat shopping list for one week:

Shopping List

Item	Cost per item	Number needed for one week	Cost for one week
wood	.50	3	1.50
Grasshopper	.30	21	6.30
berry	.10	14	1.40
water	.25	7	1.75
Acre	5.00	1	5.00
* * * * * * * * *	* * * * * * *	* * * * * * * * *	Total cost

How much will the habitat cost for one week? __$15.95__

Do you have a good habitat for a Whatsit? __yes__

How do you know? __I have everything it needs: food, shelter, water, space. maybe not friends__

Fig. 7.4. Sample Data Sheet.

Tell students that the Whatsit (in the top left corner) wants to get to its habitat (lower right corner). If the lines are roads, how many routes can it take? The Whatsit always moves toward the habitat; it never backtracks. (Answer: 24 different routes.)

CREATING YOUR OWN INVESTIGATION

This is an opportunity for students to create their own scientific study about habitats in their home environment. A sample letter to parents is provided in the Appendix to explain the student's task and instruct the parents about their role in the process.

EXTENDING

- Go back to the suggested activities, children's literature, or Rhonda's Word Play and try those you skipped, or try them again with a new twist.

- Reuse an investigation sheet at different locations, at different times of the day or year, or while on a field trip.

- Review the questions students had during the unit and make sure they are all answered.

- Have the students assemble a notebook containing all their investigations so they can see their progress as scientists. This will provide a good assessment for both you and the student, as well as something that will make everyone feel proud.

- Go to another *Nature at Your Doorstep* unit.

NATURE AT YOUR DOORSTEP
HABITAT
INVESTIGATION

Investigator _____
Date _____
Time _____
Weather _____
Study area _____

QUESTION: Can the study area provide habitats for animals? Which kinds?

HYPOTHESIS: I **think** I will find habitats for these animals: _____

_____

DATA: Fill in the chart below:

Animal	Foods	Shelters	Water Sources

CONCLUSION: I found habitats for these animals in the study area:

_____

_____

NATURE AT YOUR DOORSTEP
MAKE A COMPARISON

My comparison is between _____

_____

_____

What is the same? (*Write a sentence or draw a picture.*)

What is different? (*Write a sentence or draw a picture.*)

NATURE AT YOUR DOORSTEP
MATH CONNECTION - HABITAT

Can you design a habitat for a Whatsit?

A Whatsit needs a shelter that is 4 inches high, 4 inches wide and 4 inches deep. It eats three insects and two berries every day. It drinks one cup of water a day. It also needs 1 acre of space.

Circle the things that you would buy from each of the stores below to create a good habitat for a Whatsit.

Shelter Store

Item	Price
4" x 4" piece of wood	$0.50 each
Hay	$0.10 per handful
Brick - 4" x 2"	$0.50 each
Roof	$1.00 each

Drink Store

Item	Price
Water	$0.25 per cup
Juice	$0.35 per cup
Milk	$0.10 per cup
Soda	$0.15 per cup

Food Store

Item	Price
Berry	$0.10 each
Leaf	$0.20 each
Apple	$0.35 each
Candy Bar	$0.50 each
Hamburger	$1.00 each
Grasshopper	$0.30 each

Land Store

Item	Price
Square Foot	$2.00 each
Acre	$5.00 each
Square Yard	$3.00 each
Square Inch	$1.00 each

NATURE AT YOUR DOORSTEP
MATH CONNECTION - HABITAT

ANALYZE YOUR DATA

Create a habitat shopping list for one week:

Shopping List

Item	Cost per item	Number needed for one week	Cost for one week
* * * * * * * * * *	* * * * * * *	* * * * * * * * *	Total cost

How much will the habitat cost for one week? _____

Do you have a good habitat for a Whatsit? _____

How do you know? _____

_____

NATURE AT YOUR DOORSTEP

CREATE YOUR OWN

Investigator _____
Date _____
Time _____
Weather _____
Study area _____

(Title) _____

INVESTIGATION

QUESTION: *(What question do you have?)* _____

_____

HYPOTHESIS: *(What is your hyphothesis?)* _____

_____

DATA: *(How will you keep track of your data?)* Create your own data table:

CONCLUSION: I found _____

_____

UNIT 8

COMMUNITIES

FOCUS

Students observe plants and animals as members of a community and record the interactions they see. They then endeavor to determine the role of each member of the interaction and the effect that interaction has in the schoolyard habitat.

BACKGROUND INFORMATION

This is an investigation into the interrelationships among plants and animals that form a community. Students recognize that plants and animals exist within a context. From what they find, they deduce how various plants and animals are interacting and the effects of these interactions on both parties.

Communities are recognizable associations of plants and animals. They have various levels of organization and description. A forest community includes all the plants, animals, and fungi that regularly make the forest habitat their home. A fallen log community includes only those forest denizens directly associated with the log. Small community locales, like the log, are often referred to as *micro-habitats.* Your schoolyard might be part of an urban, suburban, or rural habitat. Micro-habitats that exist within this larger area include lawns, flower beds, drainage ditches, power line right-of-ways, sewer lines, parking lots, rooftops, and more. Each micro-habitat has its own distinct community of inhabitants. Many plants and animals are members of several micro-habitats; a few are highly restricted; and some are almost everywhere within the larger wildlife community.

Community members can have relationships closer and more involved than just sharing the same habitat. Ants and violets are members of a deciduous forest community. Close study has revealed that violet seeds are covered with a coating high in protein beneficial to ants. The ants harvest the seeds and take them to their mound, where the seed coat is eaten. The seed itself is put in the garbage chamber of the mound. This provides a perfect germination site: fertile, warm, and protected from would-be consumers. The violet germination rate in an ant mound is 90 percent, as opposed to less than 25 percent otherwise. Both the ants and the violets benefit from this association. Researchers are discovering that similar interactions among plants and animals exist in habitats all around us.

See if your class can discover a plant and animal interaction in a schoolyard community. Maybe they will make a discovery about how wildlife survives in your area.

CONNECTING COMMUNITIES

What's Happening

Give each student a copy of "Connecting Communities." (Fig. 8.1 on page 113.) Read the What's Happening section of figure 8.1 with your students. Encourage students to think about communities by asking questions such as "What makes up our human community?" "What kinds of jobs do people in our community do?" "What kinds of animals do you think live in our school community?" "What jobs do you think they have?"

Before moving on to Schoolyard Challenge, continue by building a foundation for this unit:

- Do any of the following activities. These activities work well with students of all ages.

- Read or research with your students about communities. We have included a few resources to get you started.

- Try Rhonda's Word Play. Each word play is challenging for students and is related to the topic in the unit.

Activities for Presenting Communities

- Create a list of human community members. Encourage your students to generate a list of possible interactions between two members of a community.

- Have students pretend they are animals that inhabit a schoolyard. You could interview them or have students interview each other on a tape recorder. Questions might be: What do you do all day long? What job do you do? Where do you learn how to do your job?

- Have students keep a journal about the animals they see in their schoolyard and what they see them doing.

Children's Literature

Busch, Phyllis. *At Home in Its Habitat: Animal Neighborhoods.* New York: World, 1970.

Graham, Margaret Bloy. *Be Nice to Spiders.* New York: Harper & Row, 1967.

Heller, Ruth. *The Reason for a Flower.* New York: Grosset, 1983.

Lionni, Leo. *Swimmy.* New York: Random House, 1968.

Sussman, Susan, and Robert James. *Big Friend, Little Friend: A Book About Symbiosis.* Boston: Houghton Mifflin, 1989.

Rhonda's Word Play

This Rhonda's Word Play allows students to develop their own story. The story starter is: "I walked around the corner and there stood my favorite animal. I looked at it, it looked at me, and then . . ." This is a good opportunity for drama, writing, or oral storytelling. You may want to get some of the results on tape.

Connecting Communities

What's Happening

The plants and animals that live together in an area make up a *community*. Sometimes they help each other, like bees and flowers. Sometimes they compete with each other or even hurt each other. For example, two birds may want to eat the same food, or insects can hurt a tree when they eat the wood under the bark. Plant and animal communities are studied by *ecologists*.

Schoolyard Challenge

Your challenge is to become an *ecologist* and study the way plants and animals interact in your area. Ask yourself some questions about plants and animals. Does anything happen to a tree when a squirrel builds a nest in it? Is a woodpecker helping or hurting a tree when it pecks on it?

EXTRA! Rhonda's Word Play

Can you finish this story? "I walked around the corner and there stood my favorite animal. I looked at it and it looked at me, and then . . . "

Schoolyard Challenge

Read Schoolyard Challenge with your students. Write the questions on the board or on separate chart paper for later use. Add other questions the students have about communities. Explain that you will begin answering the questions in Schoolyard Challenge today, and that you will answer the others on another day. Keep the list of questions posted in the classroom so you can add any that come up later and check off those that you investigate. Don't worry if you cannot answer the questions the students ask—research them together.

INVESTIGATING

The data collection section has four columns. (See fig. 8.2.) In the first column the plant being observed is named or drawn. In column two, students name or draw an organism that uses the plant named in column one. Column three identifies how the organism is using the plant (e.g., food, shelter, support). The last column is to hypothesize what the effect of the organism's use is on the plant.

MAKING COMPARISONS

Use this data sheet to compare interactions in various areas of the schoolyard, or interactions seen on different days, in different weather, or at different times of day.

CONNECTING MATHEMATICS

Creating a Representation

For this unit, students can create their own graphic representations of the data they collected about communities. Students will show how many plant and animal pairs they found on different days. (See fig. 8.3.)

Analyzing the Data

Follow-up questions help students think through their representations and formulate new hypotheses about when most interactions occur and why. (See fig. 8.4.) Students are also asked to notice the interactions they saw the most and hypothesize why.

Solving a Problem

Here's a community problem to solve: Butterflies, bees, and hummingbirds all like flowers. One likes big red flowers. One likes medium yellow flowers. One likes little purple flowers. Which kind of flower does each animal like? Here are some clues:

1. Hummingbirds are not in the same family as the animal who likes little purple flowers;

2. Bees' favorite flowers are bigger than butterflies' favorite flowers; and

3. The one who likes medium yellow flowers is in the same family as the butterfly.

The answer is: hummingbirds like big red flowers, bees like medium yellow flowers, and butterflies like little purple flowers.

Text continues on page 118.

NATURE AT YOUR DOORSTEP

COMMUNITIES
INVESTIGATION

Investigator _Alex_
Date _5/17_
Time _5 pm_
Weather _sunny_
Study area _patio_

QUESTION: What plants and animals will I find interacting today?

HYPOTHESIS: I **think** that I will find: _doodlebugs_ & _deadwood_ _birds_ & _trees_ ; _____ & _____ .

DATA: Draw or write what you find:

Plant	Animal	What is happening	Effect on plant
Jasmine	spider	built web	none
Salvia	caterpillar	eating leaf	losing leaf
potted cactus	centipede	living under pot	none
moss rose	bird	pooped on leaves	killing leaves
algae	tadpole	eating	none? seems to be growing bigger
oak tree	bird	resting	none

CONCLUSION: I found _many animals use plants_ _doesn't affect plants much._

Fig. 8.2. Sample Data Sheet.

NATURE AT YOUR DOORSTEP

MATH CONNECTION - COMMUNITIES

Can you create a graph showing the number of plant-animal pairs that you saw each day?

Title:

Plant and Animal Pairs

number of pairs

	Day 1	Day 2	Day 3
8			leaf & bird
7			flower & bird
6	oak tree and bird		grass & bird
5	algae and tadpole		leaf & ladybug
4	moss rose and bird		tree & bird
3	cactus and centipede	flower and ant	algae & fish
2	fern and caterpillar	oak tree and squirrel	tree and squirrel
1	jasmine spider	flower and ants	tree & beetle

Day 1 — date: 5-10, time: 5 pm, weather: cool

Day 2 — date: 5-2, time: 8:10, weather: clear

Day 3 — date: 5-11, time: 3:05, weather: cloudy

Fig. 8.3. Sample Data Sheet.

NATURE AT YOUR DOORSTEP

MATH CONNECTION - COMMUNITIES

ANALYZE YOUR DATA

Which day did you see the most plant-animal pairs? _Day 3_

What time of day was it? _3 pm_

What was the weather? _Cloudy_

Why do you think you saw the most pairs that day? _____

The park was the biggest place I looked

_____

Which day did you see the fewest plant-animal pairs? _Day 2_

What time of day was it? _8 pm_

What was the weather? _clear_

Why do you think you saw the fewest that day? _Too dark_
to see much

_____

Did you see any pair on more than one day? _Yes_

Which ones? _Tree & Squirrel, Flower & Bird_

_____

What is the total number of **different** pairs you saw in your community ?

(Be careful not to count any pairs twice) _15_

Fig. 8.4. Sample Data Sheet.

CREATING YOUR OWN INVESTIGATION

This is an opportunity for students to create their own scientific study about communities in their home environment. A sample letter to parents is provided in the Appendix to explain the student's task and invite the parents to participate in the process.

EXTENDING

- Go back to the suggested activities, children's literature, or Rhonda's Word Play and try those you skipped, or try them again with a new twist.

- Reuse the Investigation sheet at different locations, at different times of the day or year, or while on a field trip.

- Review the questions students had during the unit and make sure they are all answered.

- Have the students assemble a notebook containing all their investigations so they can see their progress as scientists. This will provide a good assessment for both you and the student, as well as something that will make everyone feel proud.

- Go to another *Nature at Your Doorstep* unit.

NATURE AT YOUR DOORSTEP
COMMUNITIES
INVESTIGATION

Investigator _____
Date _____
Time _____
Weather _____
Study area _____

QUESTION: What plants and animals will I find interacting today?

HYPOTHESIS: I **think** that I will find: _____ & _____;
_____ & _____; _____ & _____.

DATA: Draw or write what you find:

Plant	Animal	What is happening	Effect on plant

CONCLUSION: I found _____

NATURE AT YOUR DOORSTEP
MAKE A COMPARISON

My comparison is between _____

_____

_____

What is the same? (*Write a sentence or draw a picture.*)

What is different? (*Write a sentence or draw a picture.*)

NATURE AT YOUR DOORSTEP
MATH CONNECTION - COMMUNITIES

Can you create a graph showing the number of plant-animal pairs that you saw each day?

Title:_____

number of pairs

	Day 1	Day 2	Day 3
8			
7			
6			
5			
4			
3			
2			
1			

Day 1	Day 2	Day 3
date: _____	date: _____	date: _____
time: _____	time: _____	time: _____
weather: _____	weather: _____	weather: _____

NATURE AT YOUR DOORSTEP
MATH CONNECTION - COMMUNITIES

ANALYZE YOUR DATA

Which day did you see the most plant-animal pairs? _____

What time of day was it? _____

What was the weather? _____

Why do you think you saw the most pairs that day? _____

_____

_____

Which day did you see the fewest plant-animal pairs? _____

What time of day was it? _____

What was the weather? _____

Why do you think you saw the fewest that day? _____

_____

_____

Did you see any pair on more than one day? _____

Which ones? _____

_____

What is the total number of **different** pairs you saw in your community?

(Be careful not to count any pairs twice) _____

NATURE AT YOUR DOORSTEP

CREATE YOUR OWN

Investigator _____
Date _____
Time _____
Weather _____
Study area _____

(Title) _____

INVESTIGATION

QUESTION: *(What question do you have?)* _____

_____

HYPOTHESIS: *(What is your hyphothesis?)* _____

_____

DATA: *(How will you keep track of your data?)* Create your own data table:

CONCLUSION: I found _____

UNIT 9

FOOD WEBS

FOCUS

In this unit, students focus on how energy flows through their schoolyard ecosystem. Students create food webs among the various plants and animals found on the schoolyard and describe evidence that supports or disputes their hypotheses.

BACKGROUND INFORMATION

A food web illustrates some of the interrelationships among the plants and animals in an ecosystem. A major activity of all plants and animals is obtaining a share of the available food energy. Green plants, through the process of photosynthesis, are able to convert the radiant energy of the sun into carbohydrate energy. Much of the energy used by the plants goes into their growth, development, and reproduction. A small amount of it is stored in the structures of the plants. This stored energy becomes the reservoir on which the entire community depends. For this reason, green plants are often referred to as *producers*.

Animals such as mice, squirrels, deer, and grasshoppers, which eat plants (herbivores) and thus consume that stored energy, are called "primary consumers." Carnivores (e.g., cats, snakes, owls, spiders) that eat the herbivores are called *secondary consumers*.

As plants and animals die, the bulk of their stored energy is broken down by bacteria and fungi in the soil (the bacteria and fungi are sometimes called *recyclers* or *decomposers*). The simple nutrients are reused by new plants that capture more energy from the sun and keep the cycle going.

Just as plants use the vast majority of the energy they produce for their own needs, so do animals at each succeeding stage of the cycle. Less than 10 percent of the energy a plant produces or an animal consumes becomes available for the next consumer to use.

The pathways of the energy transfer from the sun through green plants to herbivores, carnivores, and bacteria and fungi are known as *food chains*. For example: grass converts radiant energy from the sun into food; a grasshopper eats the grass; a bird eats the grasshopper; a cat eats the bird. When the cat dies, its body is decomposed by bacteria and fungi, and the nutrients released become available to new plants.

This outline is a simplified version of reality. Each animal has several plants or animals (or both) on which it depends and, in turn, can provide energy to several predators.

FINDING FOOD WEBS

What's Happening

Give each student a copy of "Finding Food Webs." (Fig. 9.1 on page 127.) Read the What's Happening section of figure 9.1 with your students. Encourage students to think about food webs by asking questions such as "Can you think of an animal that eats plants?" "Can you think of an animal that eats that animal?" "Can you think of another animal that would eat that animal?" "Why do you think we need to eat animals and plants?" "Do animals and plants need food?" "Where do you think plant food comes from?"

Before moving on to Schoolyard Challenge, continue by building a foundation for this unit:

- Do any of the following activities. These activities work well with students of all ages.

- Read or research with your students about food webs. We have included a few resources to get you started.

- Try Rhonda's Word Play. Each word play is challenging for students and is related to the topic in the unit.

Activities for Presenting Food Webs

- Have students cut pictures of plants and animals out of magazines and arrange them in what they think might be a food web. Research to see if they are correct.

- Ask what the students had for breakfast or what they brought for lunch (e.g., a ham sandwich). You can then trace what they eat through what that animal eats (e.g., pigs eat corn and other plants) to make a food chain. Make several food chains this way and combine them into a food web. Is there any animal that eats people? (Mosquitoes)

- Have students make a list of the animals that they have seen either at home or at school. Let them design menus for all these animals. What would be on the menu? Take a walk and see if you can find the things on the menu.

Children's Literature

Cole, Sheila. *When the Tide Is Low.* New York: Lothrop, 1985.

Hughey, Pat. *Scavengers & Decomposers: The Cleanup Crew.* New York: Atheneum, 1984.

Lauber, Patricia. *Who Eats What? Food Chains and Food Webs.* New York: HarperCollins, 1995.

Palazzo, Janet. *Our Friend the Sun.* Mahwah, NJ: Troll, 1982.

Van Saelen, Philip. *Cricket in the Grass.* New York: Scribner's, 1979.

Rhonda's Word Play

In this word play, Rhonda is a little mixed up. Students must web together her words so they can learn something about food webs. Have your students write a sentence about their favorite animal and what it eats. Then they should cut out each word, paste them out of order on another piece of paper, and give the paper to a friend, who tries to create a logical web.

Finding Food Webs

What's Happening

Plants and animals are growing! Growing takes a lot of *energy*. Plants get their energy from the sun and soak up extra nutrition from the ground. Animals get their energy by eating plants or other animals. When we link together an animal with the plants or animals it eats and with the animals that eat it, we make a *food chain*. If we put together several food chains connecting plants and animals from one community or habitat, we make a *food web*.

Schoolyard Challenge

Your challenge is to become a food web expert for your area. Using some of the animals and plants from your biodiversity or community study, you will put together a food web. Ask yourself some questions that will help you find the food web connections. Which animals in this group eat plants? Which ones eat other animals? Will one animal be connected to one plant or many plants?

EXTRA! Rhonda's Word Play

Can you connect these words to make a sentence about food webs?

energy
live   Plants
need   to   and
animals

Schoolyard Challenge

Read Schoolyard Challenge with your students. Write the questions on the board or on separate chart paper for later use. Add other questions the students have about food webs. Explain that you will answer the questions in the Schoolyard Challenge today and will answer the others on another day. Keep the list of questions posted in the classroom so you can add any that come up later and check off those that you investigate. Don't worry if you cannot answer the questions the students ask—research them together.

INVESTIGATING

On this Investigation sheet, students will choose a set of 14 plants and animals from their biodiversity or community Investigation sheet that they think may form a food web. They will then place one plant or animal in each box on the Investigation sheet and draw lines connecting all the pairs they believe are linked in a food chain. Those pairs will appear on the second part of the form. (See figs. 9.2 and 9.3.) Students will search the study area for evidence to support or dispute their hypotheses.

The conclusion for this sheet is to list those pairs for which supporting evidence was found. Students can make one class food web with all the connections found by the class members.

MAKING COMPARISONS

In this study, compare your hypothesis to your data and compare the food webs you find on different days, at alternate times of the year, and in various sites. Also, use this as an opportunity to begin the math connection section where students will be working with Venn diagrams.

CONNECTING MATHEMATICS

Creating a Representation

Students will create Venn diagrams by deciding which animals they found are herbivores, carnivores, or omnivores. (See fig. 9.4.) Extend this activity by having students make a different kind of representation with the same information, or think of other sets of information and try to make new Venn diagrams.

Students can also categorize the organisms they have found as Producers, green plants that produce their own food using energy from the sun; Consumers (Herbivores), animals that eat plants or fungi or both; Consumers (Carnivores), organisms that eat animals (these are generally animals, but there are a few carnivorous plants); or Decomposers, organisms such as termites or fungi that get energy from dead plant and animal material. Using these categories, let the students determine whether there are any patterns in the order of energy flow from the sun through the ecological community.

Analyzing the Data

Follow-up questions in this section allow students to think about the data they collected by reviewing their representation. (See fig. 9.5.) Older students can write their own answers, or you can use these questions for discussion purposes.

Text continues on page 133.

NATURE AT YOUR DOORSTEP

FOOD WEB
INVESTIGATION

Investigator _Ellen Davis_
Date _5/11/96_
Time _3:50_
Weather _sunny_
Study area _park_

QUESTION: What food web exists in the study area?

HYPOTHESIS: I **think** that these plants and animals make up a food web in the study area:

Draw or name a plant or animal from your biodiversity investigation in each box. Draw a line connecting each pair you think make up a link in the food web.

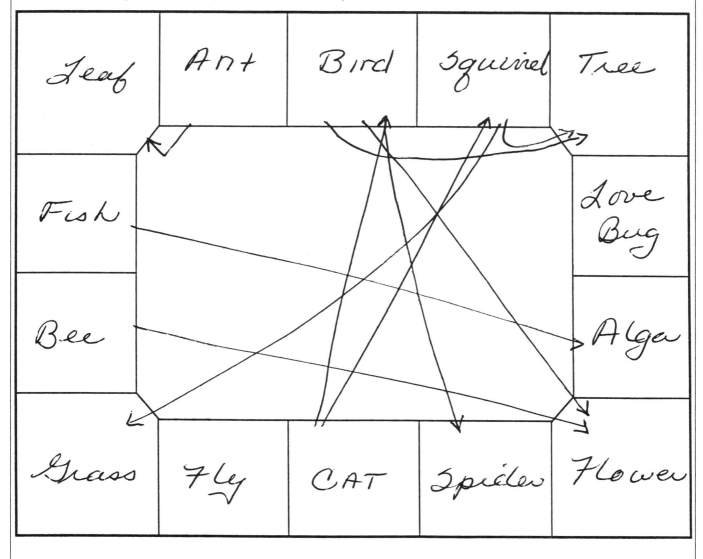

Fig. 9.2. Sample Data Sheet.

NATURE AT YOUR DOORSTEP

DATA: Write the evidence you find that supports or disputes the web connections in your hypothesis:

Connected pair	Evidence	Support/ Disprove
Fish/Algae	Goldfish in and around algae in pond	support
Bee/Flower	A bee in a flower	suppot
Grass/Squirrel	Squirrel carrying grass	"
Cat/Bird	Cat watching bird	"
Flower/Bird	Hummingbird in flower	"
Spider/Bird		NONE
Tree/Squirrel	Squirrel in a tree w/nut	support
Tree/Bird		None

CONCLUSION: I found _support for most of my hypotheses - But no evidence for_

Fig. 9.3. Sample Data Sheet.

NATURE AT YOUR DOORSTEP

MATH CONNECTION - FOOD WEBS

Can you create a Venn diagram with the data you collected?

Try using **herbivores** (plant eaters), **carnivores** (meat eaters) and **omnivores** (plant and meat eaters)

My title: _____ Eaters _____

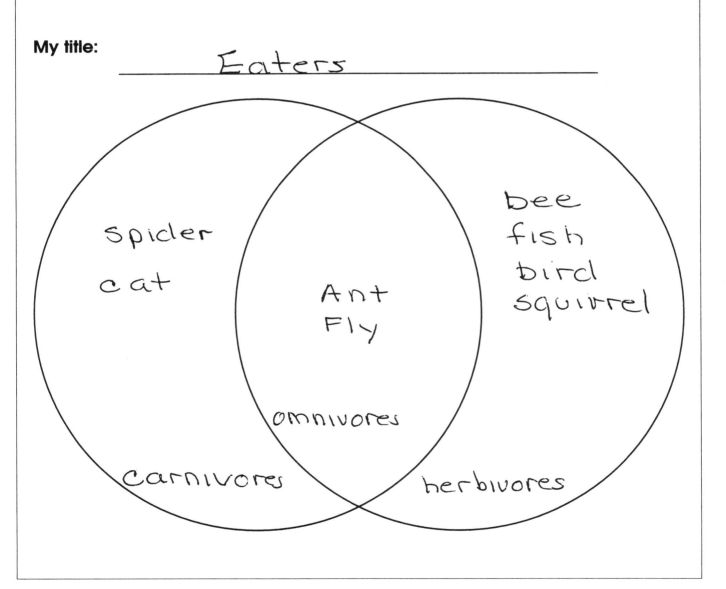

Fig. 9.4. Sample Data Sheet.

NATURE AT YOUR DOORSTEP

MATH CONNECTION - FOOD WEBS

ANALYZE YOUR DATA

How many herbivores did you find? _____4_____

How many herbivores do you think there might be in the study area?

_____at least 20_____

How many carnivores did you find? _____2_____

How many carnivores do you think there might be in the study area?

_____maybe 10_____

Did you find any animals that are both carnivores and herbivores

(omnivores)? __yes__ - ants, flies

_____

Why do you think some animals eat both plants and animals? _____

_____more choices for food_____

_____better diet_____

What do you think would happen to a habitat that had more carni-

vores than herbivores? They might eat up all the herbivores

What do you think would happen to a habitat that had more herbi-

vores than carnivores? They might eat up all the plants

Fig. 9.5. Sample Data Sheet.

Solving a Problem

Approximately 10 percent of the energy a plant produces or an animal consumes becomes available for the next consumer to use. Suppose a plant that has consumed energy from the sun is eaten by an insect; and the insect is eaten by a bird; and the bird is eaten by an opossum; and the opossum is eaten by a coyote. What percentage of the sun's energy originally absorbed by the plant is consumed by the coyote? Answer: 1/100 of a percent.

CREATING YOUR OWN INVESTIGATION

This is an opportunity for students to create their own scientific study about food webs in their home environment. A sample letter to parents is provided in the Appendix to explain the student's task and instruct the parents about their role in the process.

EXTENDING

- Go back to the suggested activities, children's literature, or Rhonda's Word Play and try those you skipped, or try them again with a new twist.

- Reuse the investigation sheet at different locations, at different times of the day or year, or while on a field trip.

- Review the questions students had during the unit and make sure they are all answered.

- Have the students assemble a notebook containing all their investigations so they can see their progress as scientists. This will provide a good assessment for both you and the students, as well as something that will make everyone feel proud.

- Go to another *Nature at Your Doorstep* unit.

NATURE AT YOUR DOORSTEP
FOOD WEB
INVESTIGATION

Investigator _____
Date _____
Time _____
Weather _____
Study area _____

QUESTION: What food web exists in the study area?

HYPOTHESIS: I **think** that these plants and animals make up a food web in the study area:

Draw or name a plant or animal from your biodiversity investigation in each box. Draw a line connecting each pair you think make up a link in the food web.

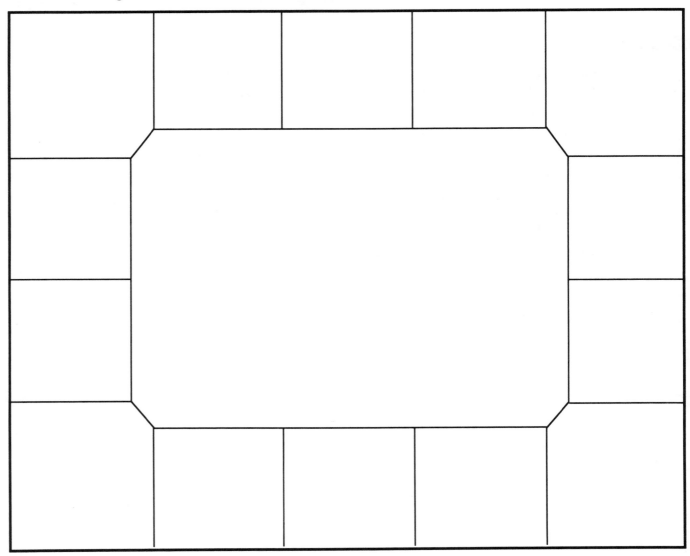

NATURE AT YOUR DOORSTEP

DATA: *Write the evidence you find that supports or disputes the web connections in your hypothesis:*

Connected pair	Evidence	Support/ Dispute

CONCLUSION: I found _____

_____

_____

NATURE AT YOUR DOORSTEP
MAKE A COMPARISON

My comparison is between _____

_____

_____

What is the same? *(Write a sentence or draw a picture.)*

What is different? *(Write a sentence or draw a picture.)*

NATURE AT YOUR DOORSTEP
MATH CONNECTION - FOOD WEBS

Can you create a Venn diagram with the data you collected?

Try using **herbivores** (plant eaters), **carnivores** (meat eaters) and **omnivores** (plant and meat eaters)

Title:

_____

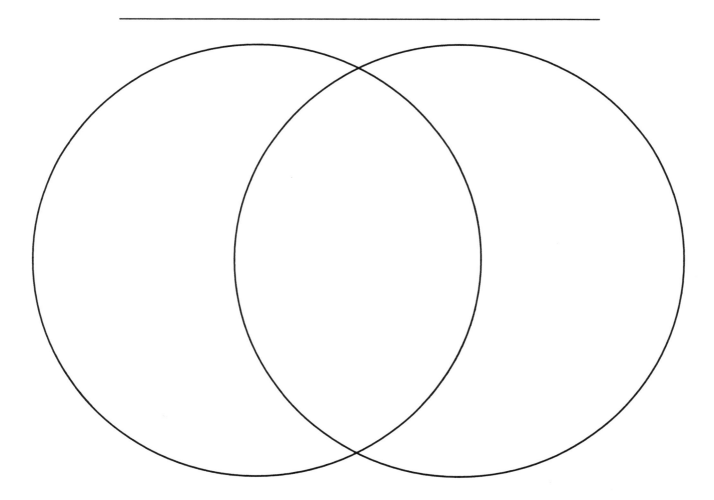

NATURE AT YOUR DOORSTEP
MATH CONNECTION - FOOD WEBS

ANALYZE YOUR DATA

How many herbivores did you find? _____

How many herbivores do you think there might be in the study area?

_____

How many carnivores did you find? _____

How many carnivores do you think there might be in the study area?

_____

Did you find any animals that are both carnivores and herbivores

(omnivores)? _____

_____

Why do you think some animals eat both plants and animals? _____

_____

_____

What do you think would happen to a habitat that had more carni-

vores than herbivores? _____

_____

What do you think would happen to a habitat that had more herbi-

vores than carnivores? _____

_____

NATURE AT YOUR DOORSTEP

CREATE YOUR OWN

Investigator _____

(Title) _____

Date _____
Time _____
Weather _____
Study area _____

INVESTIGATION

QUESTION: *(What question do you have?)* _____

_____

HYPOTHESIS: *(What is your hyphothesis?)* _____

_____

DATA: *(How will you keep track of your data?)* Create your own data table:

CONCLUSION: I found _____

_____

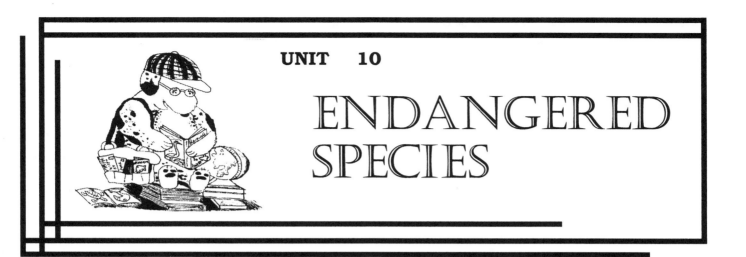

UNIT 10

ENDANGERED SPECIES

FOCUS

Inevitably, students will make decisions that will affect the natural resources of their community. They must not only understand that there are endangered plant and animal species, but also the processes that result in species becoming endangered. Students transfer knowledge gained in at least four previous units—habitats, communities, biodiversity, and food webs—to give them insights about why a species becomes endangered and the difficulties associated with trying to preserve it. Supplying this opportunity in their schoolyard gives students a meaningful context.

BACKGROUND INFORMATION

The subject of endangered species is one of the most popular and controversial areas of biology. Because it is generally accepted that biodiversity is important, any reduction in biodiversity is considered a critical problem. Although extinction is a natural part of evolution, it would be offset naturally by the emergence of new species. The reason for concern is the rapid rate of extinction currently occurring worldwide. This rapid rate is caused in part by the actions of humans and their society. Humans are radically changing the environment faster than animals can adapt. These animals become endangered as their populations become critically low. If these low populations are not identified, protected, and bolstered, the species eventually will become extinct.

Some human activities, such as poaching, directly endanger some animals. Other seemingly harmless activities can be indirectly devastating to other animals. Cattle ranching, for example, clears forests for pastures, sets up stock tanks, and creates fences, providing an ideal habitat for cowbirds. The cowbirds' habit of laying eggs in songbird nests contributes to the decrease of songbird populations.

Every alteration of the environment affects other species. Humans know so little of how plants and animals interact that we usually do not realize that we have affected an environment until something becomes abnormally abundant or rare. Future generations will have much more information about the proper care of the environment, and they will need to understand how species become endangered and the effect that extinction of one species has on the environment as a whole.

ENDEARING ENDANGERED SPECIES

What's Happening

Give each student a copy of "Endearing Endangered Species." (Fig. 10.1 on pages 143-44.) Read the What's Happening section of figure 10.1 with your students. Encourage students to think about endangered species by asking questions such as "Can you think of a plant or animal that is an endangered species?" "What do you think endangered means?" "Why do you think that species become endangered?"

Before moving on to Schoolyard Challenge, continue building a foundation for this unit:

- Do any of the following activities. These activities work well with students of all ages.

- Read or research with your students about endangered species. We have included a few resources to get you started.

- Try Rhonda's Word Play. Each word play is challenging for students and is related to the topic in the unit.

Activities for Presenting Endangered Species

- Build a pyramid or other tall structure with blocks to represent an ecosystem. Pull blocks from the structure one at a time to represent species that become extinct. How many can you pull out before the entire structure falls down?

- Have students make a circle. Count off by fours. Ones represent food, twos represent water, threes represent shelter, and fours represent space. Form a complete circle by having students sit on each others' laps. Tap one on the shoulder to leave the circle. How long will the circle last?

Children's Literature

Brown, Mary Barrett. *Wings Along the Waterway*. New York: Orchard, 1992.

Burningham, John. *Hey! Get Off Our Train*. New York: Crown, 1989.

Cherry, Lynn. *A River Ran Wild*. San Diego, CA: Harcourt Brace, 1992.

Mattson, Mark. *Environmental Atlas of the United States*. New York: Scholastic, 1993.

Wood, Douglas. *Old Turtle*. Duluth, MN: Pfeifer-Hamilton, 1992.

Wright, Alexandra. *Will We Miss Them? Endangered Species*. Watertown, MA: Charlesbridge, 1992.

Van Allsburg, Chris. *Just a Dream*. Boston: Houghton Mifflin, 1990.

Rhonda's Word Play

Rhonda has presented the names of a number of endangered species. It's a little difficult to read them because a letter is missing in each set of words. Students are asked to find the missing (endangered) letter so that Rhonda's information makes sense. Have students write their own endangered species with a letter missing. Trade papers and see if their partners can figure it out. If students are unfamiliar with a particular animal or plant species, try finding a picture of it.

Endearing Endangered Species

What's Happening

Some kinds (*species*) of plants and animals are dying out. If all the members of a species die, that species becomes *extinct*. That means they are gone forever. Dinosaurs and tree ferns are examples of species that have become extinct. Some plants and animals are having such a hard time finding what they need to live that fewer and fewer of them survive. Sometimes their habitat changes, their water becomes polluted, or their food becomes poisoned. Sometimes new plants or animals move in and take over. When these things happen, that species becomes *endangered*. That means that it is in danger of becoming extinct.

Many kinds of scientists study endangered plants and animals. What kind of scientist will you be for this study?

_____

_____

NATURE AT YOUR DOORSTEP

Schoolyard Challenge

Your challenge is to find out why a plant or animal that lives or used to live in your area is endangered. You will learn about that species and use your earlier studies to help you find out why the population is dropping. Ask yourself some questions about how your species has become endangered. Does this habitat still have enough space? Are there other plant or animal members of the community that are missing now?

EXTRA! Rhonda's Word Play

All of the following jumble of letters are plants and animals on the endangered species list. Can you figure out which letter of the alphabet is missing in each species name and put it in so you will learn the names of these species?

Plants	Mammals	Birds	Reptiles
Blck Lce Cctus	Bue Whae	Bad Eage	Grn Sa Turtl
Texas Wld Rce	lack ear	Sptted wl	Spckld Racr

_____   _____   _____   _____

_____   _____   _____   _____

Schoolyard Challenge

Read Schoolyard Challenge with your students. Write the questions on the board or on separate chart paper for later use. Add any questions the students have about endangered species. Explain that the questions in the Schoolyard Challenge are the questions you will begin answering today, and that you will answer the others another day. Keep the list of questions posted in the classroom so you can add any that come up later and check off those that you investigate. Don't worry if you cannot answer the questions the students ask—just research them together.

INVESTIGATING

This unit is an excellent culmination and potential assessment of the students' comprehension of and ability to work with the information in the previous units. Review the concepts from *Habitats*, *Communities*, *Biodiversity*, and *Food Webs*. Focus on the factors necessary for an organism's existence. Have the students either research organisms once common to your area or choose a creature from a local list of endangered or threatened plants and animals (these can be acquired from your state department of natural resources). Individuals or teams should choose a plant or animal that has *not* appeared in their studies. Their goal in this investigation is to identify the factors that have contributed to the organism's extinction in the study area.

1. Habitat: the students will identify (possibly through research) the food, shelter, water, and space necessary for their organism's survival.

2. Biodiversity/Communities: the students will seek any particular plants or animals upon which their organism is dependent (communities in which it is often a part).

3. Food Webs: students will identify the organism's food sources and consumers necessary to keep its population within bounds.

Using the information above, the students will revisit the study site and determine which of these components are not present, or exist in insufficient quantities. They will also note other factors (e.g., introduced, potentially competitive species; pollution) that could pose a problem for their study subject. (See figs. 10.2 and 10.3.)

In conclusion, the students will state the factors they have identified that affect the existence of their study organism.

MAKING COMPARISONS

A number of comparisons can be made. Students can compare their organism's current habitat with its ideal habitat. Or two students can compare the endangered animals' habitat with the habitat of a nonendangered animal that was found on the site.

CONNECTING MATHEMATICS

Creating a Representation

Students are asked to create a line graph showing how the population of their plant or animal has changed since they were born. (See fig. 10.4.) This will take some research. A call to your local or state national resource department should prove helpful.

Text continues on page 149.

NATURE AT YOUR DOORSTEP

ENDANGERED SPECIES
INVESTIGATION

Investigator ___Jay___
Date ___4-10-95___
Time ___10 AM___
Weather ___sunny___
Study area ___park___

Study organism ___Attwater Prairie Chicken___

QUESTION: What factors have affected this organism's ability to live here?

HYPOTHESIS: I **think** the main factors are: ___space___

_____

_____

DATA: Use information from your previous investigations and your research to fill in the data boxes below. Then visit your study area.

A. Habitat- _Write the food, shelter, water and space requirements of your organism. Check the ones that_ **are** _fulfilled by the study area._

Food	here?	Shelter	here?
seeds	Y	tall grass	N
insects	Y	grass nest in grass	N

Water	here?	Space	here?
not much	Y	prairie	N
		courtship area	?

Fig. 10.2. Sample Data Sheet.

NATURE AT YOUR DOORSTEP

B. Communities - *Write the plants and animals that your organism interacts with. Check those that **do** exist in the study area.*

Community plants and animals	Is it here?
tall grass prairie	No
bunch grass	No

C. Food Webs - *Write the food sources and the predators of your organism. Check off the ones you **do** find in the study area.*

Foods	here?	Predators	here?
seeds	Y	hawks	Y
insects	Y	coyotes	Y
		snakes	N

CONCLUSION: The main factors are <u>Prairie grasses</u> <u>for nesting , space</u>

_____

_____

Fig. 10.3. Sample Data Sheet.

NATURE AT YOUR DOORSTEP

MATH CONNECTION - ENDANGERED SPECIES

Can you create a line graph showing how the population of your study organism has changed since you were born?

Title:

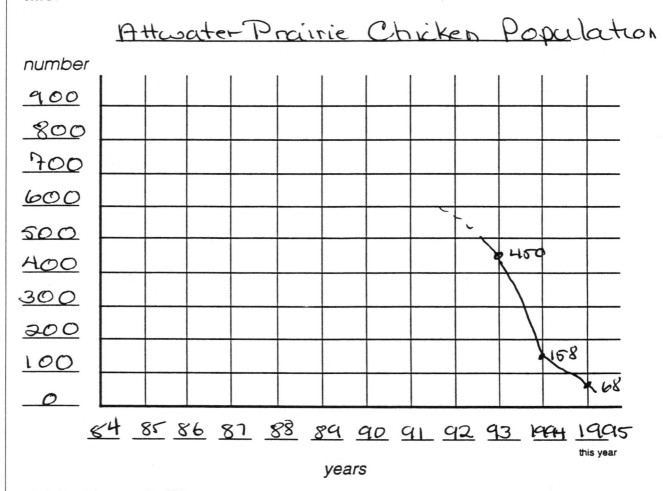

Attwater Prairie Chicken Population

number

900
800
700
600
500
400 o 450
300
200
100 ⟨158
0   ⟨68

84 85 86 87 88 89 90 91 92 93 1994 1995

this year

years

ANALYZE YOUR DATA

What percent of the first year's population is the current population? __15%__

Is there a trend in the change in the population since you were born? __yes__

If so, what is the trend? __The population is going down__

Fig. 10.4. Sample Data Sheet.

Analyzing the Data

Students are asked a series of questions relative to their data. (See fig. 10.5.) They will need to determine percentages or differences of population between the year they were born and the current year. They will also be asked to make a conclusion about the trend of the line they have created. Is it up or down?

Solving a Problem

Students will now solve the problem of determining a plan of action that would allow their organism to exist in the study area. These plans may not be feasible; if the study organism is an American Bison, for example, the plan would likely include purchasing several thousand acres of land to support a herd large enough to be sustained. However, from these plans you may find some that could be put into practice, such as planting flowers that will attract and support a particular butterfly. After changes are made, you can restudy the area to discover what other changes have occurred, some of which may be unexpected.

CREATING YOUR OWN INVESTIGATION

This is an opportunity for students to create their own scientific study about endangered species in their home environment. A sample letter to parents is provided in the Appendix to explain the student's task and instruct the parents about their role in the process.

EXTENDING

- Go back to the suggested activities, children's literature, or Rhonda's Word Play and try those you skipped, or try them again with a new twist.

- Review the questions students had during the unit and make sure they are all answered.

- Go back to another *Nature at Your Doorstep* unit.

NATURE AT YOUR DOORSTEP

TAKE ACTION !

How could you provide the proper conditions for your study organism to return to your site?

What kinds of foods (plants and animals) would need to be added to the habitat? _none_

_____

What types of shelter places and materials would need to be added to the habitat? _____
tall grass, prairie grass

What types of water sources would need to be added to the habitat? _____

_____

How much space would be needed for your organism? _____
At least a square mile

Are there other plants or animals that your organism interacts with that need to be added to the

habitat? _prairie grasses_ _____

_____

Would any predators be needed to keep your organism's population under control? _no_

Which ones? _____

Could those predators survive in this habitat? _____

****

Would it be possible to create a suitable habitat for your study organism? _Maybe for 2_

Why or Why not? _not enough space in the park for nests. Not the right kind of grass. Too many people_

Fig. 10.5. Sample Data Sheet.

NATURE AT YOUR DOORSTEP
ENDANGERED SPECIES
INVESTIGATION

Investigator _____
Date _____
Time _____
Weather _____
Study area _____

Study organism _____

QUESTION: What factors have affected this organism's ability to live here?

HYPOTHESIS: I **think** the main factors are: _____
_____
_____

DATA: Use information from your previous investigations and your research to fill in the data boxes below. Then visit your study area.

A. Habitat- *Write the food, shelter, water and space requirements of your organism. Check the ones that* **are** *fulfilled by the study area.*

Food	here?	Shelter	here?

Water	here?	Space	here?

NATURE AT YOUR DOORSTEP

B. Communities - *Write the plants and animals that your organism interacts with. Check those that **do** exist in the study area.*

Community plants and animals	Is it here?

C. Food Webs - *Write the food sources and the predators of your organism. Check off the ones you **do** find in the study area.*

Foods	here?	Predators	here?

CONCLUSION: The main factors are _____

_____

_____

_____

NATURE AT YOUR DOORSTEP
MAKE A COMPARISON

My comparison is between _____

_____

_____

What is the same? (*Write a sentence or draw a picture.*)

What is different? (*Write a sentence or draw a picture.*)

NATURE AT YOUR DOORSTEP
MATH CONNECTION - ENDANGERED SPECIES

Can you create a line graph showing how the population of your study organism has changed since you were born?

Title:

_____

number

this year

years

ANALYZE YOUR DATA

What percent of the first year's population is the current population? _____

Is there a trend in the change in the population since you were born? _____

If so, what is the trend? _____

NATURE AT YOUR DOORSTEP
TAKE ACTION !

How could you provide the proper conditions for your study organism to return to your site?

What kinds of foods (plants and animals) would need to be added to the habitat? _____

_____

What types of shelter places and materials would need to be added to the habitat? _____

_____

What types of water sources would need to be added to the habitat? _____

_____

How much space would be needed for your organism? _____

_____

Are there other plants or animals that your organism interacts with that need to be added to the

habitat? _____

_____

Would any predators be needed to keep your organism's population under control? _____

Which ones? _____

Could those predators survive in this habitat? _____

****

Would it be possible to create a suitable habitat for your study organism? _____

Why or Why not? _____

_____

_____

_____

NATURE AT YOUR DOORSTEP

CREATE YOUR OWN

(Title)_____

INVESTIGATION

Investigator _____
Date _____
Time _____
Weather _____
Study area _____

QUESTION: *(What question do you have?)* _____

_____

HYPOTHESIS: *(What is your hyphothesis?)* _____

_____

DATA: *(How will you keep track of your data?)* Create your own data table:

CONCLUSION: I found _____

_____

REFERENCES

American Forest Council. *Project Learning Tree.* Washington, DC: American Forest Council, 1993.

Baker, Ann, and Johnny Baker. *Counting on a Small Planet.* Portsmouth, NH: Heinemann, 1991.

Basile, Carole. "The Effects of an Outdoor Nature Investigation Program on Young Children's Ability to Transfer Knowledge." University of Houston, Doctoral Dissertation, 1996.

Bowder, Marcia. *Nature for the Very Young.* New York: John Wiley, 1989.

Cornell, Joseph. *Sharing Nature with Children.* Nevada City, CA: Dawn, 1989.

Freedman, Robin. *Open-Ended Questioning.* Menlo Park, CA: Addison-Wesley, 1994.

Herman, Marina. *Teaching Kids to Love the Earth.* Duluth, MN: Pfeifer-Hamilton, 1991.

Hillman, Lawrence. *Nature Puzzlers.* Englewood, CO: Teacher Ideas Press, 1989.

International Reading Association and National Council of Teachers of English. *Standards for the English Language Arts.* Newark, DE: International Reading Association. Urbana, IL: National Council of Teachers of English, 1996.

Johns, Frank, Kurt Liske, and Amy Evans. *Education Goes Outdoors.* Reading, MA: Addison-Wesley, 1986.

Lingelbach, Jennifer. *Hands-On Nature.* Woodstock, VT: Vermont Institute of Natural Science, 1986.

Murdoch, Kathy. *Ideas of Environmental Education in Elementary Classrooms.* Portsmouth, NH: Heinemann, 1995.

National Council for the Social Studies. *Curriculum Standards for Social Studies.* Washington, DC: National Council for the Social Studies, 1994.

National Council for the Teaching of Mathematics. *Curriculum and Evaluation Standards for School Mathematics.* Reston, VA: National Council for the Teaching of Mathematics, 1989.

National Research Council. *National Science Education Standards*. Washington, DC: National Academy Press, 1996.

Russell, Helen Ross. *Ten-Minute Field Trips*. Washington, DC: National Science Teachers Association, 1993.

Sheehan, Kathy, and Mary Waidner. *Earthchild*. Tulsa, OK: Council Oak, 1991.

Sisson, Edith. *Nature with Children of All Ages*. Englewood Cliffs, NJ: Prentice Hall, 1982.

Western Regional Environmental Education Council. *Project WILD*. Austin, TX: Western Regional Environmental Education Council, 1992.

APPENDIX

LETTER TO PARENTS

Dear Parents/Guardian,

Our class has been studying exciting subjects in science this year. Using a program called *Nature at Your Doorstep*, your child is learning many things about the plants and animals that live in our area, most of them right in our own schoolyard.

In our investigations, students use their senses to investigate topics that range from trees to endangered species. Our class is currently investigating _____ . Students are developing their own questions, creating their own hypotheses, and analyzing their own data. We have already done this in our schoolyard, and now students are looking forward to continuing their investigations at home.

To help the students try their investigations again at home, I have given them a data sheet called "Create Your Own Investigation." The child can investigate whatever he or she would like either using a method we have practiced in school or coming up with something new.

In addition, here is an activity you can do at home with your child regarding the topic we are studying, plus references to related children's literature that she or he might enjoy:

(Choose from any of the suggested activities we have provided or activities from other sources.)
(Choose from any of the literature references provided or one of your favorites.)

Your help and encouragement is appreciated. I look forward to your participation in our science program this year. If you have any questions about this activity, please feel free to contact me. Let's work together to help your child succeed in science!

Yours truly,

ABOUT THE AUTHORS

Carole G. Basile, shown on right in picture below, has an Ed.D. in Curriculum and Instruction from the University of Houston. Her specialization is teaching science and mathematics to young children. Dr. Basile is the recipient of the 1995 University of Houston's Teaching Excellence Award and is currently teaching early childhood educators at the University of Houston.

Jennifer Gillespie-Malone, center, graduated from the University of Rochester, NY, and has a master's degree from UCLA. She is currently an Education Specialist at the Hana and Arthur Ginzbarg Nature Discovery Center in Bellaire, TX. She has taught in various settings, from grass huts in the Micronesian islands to universities and museums in Canada, the United States, and the Netherlands.

Fred Collins, left, a native Houstonian, is a wildlife graduate of Texas A&M University where he also attended graduate school. In addition to his full-time position as Director of the Nature Discovery Center, he does consulting as an endangered species biologist. He and his wife of 25 years maintain a flock of more than 30 species of parrots at his Center for Avian Propagation and Research.

from Teacher Ideas Press

Beyond the Bean Seed: Gardening Activities for Grades K–6
Nancy Allen Jurenka and Rosanne J. Blass

Engaging book-based lessons integrate gardening, children's literature, and language arts through creative activities embellished with poetry, word play, and recipes. The projects lead to learning in a variety of other subjects—from ecology, history, and geography to career exploration and the sciences. **Grades K–6**.
xiv, 195p. 8½x11 paper ISBN 1-56308-346-9

Cultivating a Child's Imagination Through Gardening
Nancy Allen Jurenka and Rosanne J. Blass

Each of these 45 lessons focuses on a specific book about gardening and offers related activities such as reading, writing, poetry, word play, music, dancing, dramatics, and other activities to enhance creativity and build literacy skills. A great companion to *Beyond the Bean Seed*. **Grades K–6**.
xiv, 143p. 8½x11 paper ISBN 1-56308-452-X

Science Through Children's Literature: An Integrated Approach
Carol M. Butzow and John W. Butzow

This best-seller provides instructional units that integrate all areas of the curriculum and serve as models to educators at all levels. Adopted by schools of education nationwide, it features more than 30 outstanding children's fiction books that are rich in scientific concepts yet equally well known for their strong story lines and universal appeal. **Grades K–3**.
xviii, 234p. 8½x11 paper ISBN 0-87287-667-5

Primary Dinosaur Investigations: How We Know What We Know
Craig A. Munsart and Karen Alonzi Van Gundy

Take students from a fascination with dinosaurs to science success with delightful dinosaur-based activities that teach them to think like scientists. This introductory teachers' guide is packed with classroom-ready, teacher-friendly, student-tested activities that will engage students and help them develop critical-thinking and research skills. **Grades K–3**.
xxi, 293p. 8½x11 paper ISBN 1-56308-246-2

Glues, Brews, and Goos: Recipes and Formulas for Almost Any Classroom Project
Diana F. Marks

Pulling together hundreds of practical, easy recipes and formulas for classroom projects—from paints and salt map mixtures to volcanic action concoctions—these kid-tested projects make learning authentic and enjoyable. All projects use ingredients that are easy to find and processes that are up-to-date. Tips on when, why, and how to use these terrific concoctions are also included. **Grades K–6**.
xvi, 179p. 8½x11 paper ISBN 1-56308-362-0

Appreciating Diversity Through Children's Literature:
Teaching Activities for the Primary Grades
Meredith McGowan, Patricia J. Wheeler, and Tom McGowan

Incorporating literature about diverse people into the curriculum encourages students to comprehend and value diversity. In this resource, stories that focus on four areas of diversity—age, gender, physical abilities, and ethnicity—provide the basis for activities that encourage children to think, empathize, and take action. **Grades 1–3**.
xvii, 135p. 8½x11 paper ISBN 1-56308-117-2

For a FREE catalog or to order any of our titles, please contact:
Teacher Ideas Press
Dept. B26 • P.O. Box 6633 • Englewood, CO 80155-6633
Phone: 1-800-237-6124 • Fax: 303-220-8843 • E-mail: lu-books@lu.com